EMERGING ISSUES ON GENDER AND WOMEN DEVELOPMENT

EMERGING ISSUES ON GENDER AND WOMEN DEVELOPMENT

PROF. K. ELANGO
DR. A. AYYAM PERUMAL
PROF. J. MOHAN RAJ

ABHIJEET PUBLICATIONS
DELHI 110094

ABHIJEET PUBLICATIONS
2/46 Tukhmeerpur Extension
Delhi-110 094
Phone: 011-22960492, 65698474
E-mail: abhijeetpublication@gmail.com

EMERGING ISSUES ON GENDER AND WOMEN DEVELOPMENT

First Published 2008

ISBN 978-81-89886-67-7

PRINTED IN INDIA

Published by J.K. Singh for Abhijeet Publications, Delhi-110 094, Lasertypeset by Gaurav Graphics, New Delhi and Printed at Himanshu Printers, Delhi.

Dedicated to
Our Beloved Parents

Preface

Women are placed on a pride position in the society and in religion. The part played by women in the modern society is inevitable in all parts of the society. Our religions like, Hindu, Muslim, Christianity and Jains, gave much importance to them as "Holy Mother". This book makes an attempt to show the gender equality and poverty reduction in the developing arena. It also shows women rights, women empowerment through SHG, women's agency in power building women atrocities and also shows the related issues of women.

First of all I place my sincere thank to our Most Respected Secretary and Correspondent Advocate Sri S. RAGUNATHAN and other members of the College council for their moral support in bringing out this book in an efficient manner.

I owe my affectionate thanks to Dr. C. THANGAMUTHU Former Vice-Chancellor of Bharathidasan University for his constant encouragement.

Again I place my thanks to Dr. K. ANBARASU Msc. M.Phil. Ph.D. Principal National College for his enthuastic support.

Words are inadequate to express my affectionate thank to Prof. S.X. PRABU, M.A., M.Phil., Head of the Department of Economics and other learned professors for their support.

I place my heart felt thanks to Dr. T. SEMBAN, Head of the Department of Economics, Urumu Dhanalakshmi College and my beloved wife S. SUSEELA, B.A.

Again I owe my thank to Dr. A. AYYAM PERUMAL and his wife and his uncle Mr. M. ARUNACHALAM.

Mrs. A. MALATHI SRI AKILA & CO., TRICHY for their excellent help in all stages.

Suggestions are welcome.

I leave it to the Readers.

K. ELANGO

Contents

Contents

1

Changes in Livelihoods of Women Economic Activity

Women in India is considered as a holy and pious symbol. To give topmost importance in the society is dating from in immemorial period. Great Epics Like Ramayana, and Mahabharata women are considered as a worshipful and spiritual Goddess. In India Goddess Saraswathi, Lakshmi, Parvathi, Ganga, Kali and Mariyamman are the prominent examples. Women is considered as a inevitable and essential part in our society for that purpose alone we call; In everyman's success there will be a women behind him.

Development effectiveness through gender mainstreaming signifies performance in bringing about change in increased productivity, improved social development and enhanced gender equality in rights, resources and political voice that generally disadvantage women. The costs of gender inequality are particularly noted in hindering development in terms of more poverty, increased deprivation and chronic failure in satisfaction of social needs (nutrition, health, education, dignity, social prestige, self-esteem). Thus, development effectiveness cannot be measured exclusively in terms of reduction of income poverty, or in the achievement of project objectives. One must also focus on the impact of development assistance on processes of inclusion, enhancing capabilities and gender/social equalities.

To assess the effectiveness of a given development intervention, two questions need to be answered in tandem. What contribution does development policy make to bring about change in gendered conditions for achieving reduction of poverty and women's inequality? What policies or programmes have been effective in closing the gap between development rhetoric and the reality of women's day to day existence; and in setting new standards for gender-responsibility of public accountability system, including that of the civil society?

Since the mid-1990s, there has been a major research effort into development effectiveness by academics around the world. A 1997 desk review of the World Bank projects found that projects that took gender relations into account in their design and implementation tended to achieve their objectives more often than projects that ignored gender issues [Murphy 1997].

This was further supported by a more recent analysis done by the Bank, based on desk reviews and field studies. This analysis concluded that projects tended to have better on-the-ground impact when gender issues had been analysed at the country and Project levels and gender-differentiated needs or impacts were recognized in project and programme design [World Bank 2001]. In India, for example, "The simulation results suggest that the two interventions most strongly associated with infant mortality Reduction in the poor states are increased schooling of mothers and additional public spending on health and family welfare" [Deolalikar 2005:3]. That failures to recognize ... gender-differentiated constraints when designing policies can compromise the effectiveness of those policies, from both equity and efficiency perspectives" [World Bank 2001:14].

If development projects, and project officials, do not take the lead in initiating measures to reduce present inequalities in gender relations, such changes are not likely to come about on their own, through so-called demand-driven measure, given that the men who dominate the social sphere would inevitably dominate the formulation of demand-driven measures. Project design and implementation by project officials are necessary to ensure that the much-needed social changes, changes in gender relations, are made a part of poverty reductions process.

Gender Inequality and Poverty

A large number of reviews during 1999 to 2004 noted that throughout south Asia, countries have improved their development policies as reflected in trends in a number of sectoral and thematic analyses. The most noticeable improvement occurred in policies related to gender and efficiency of resource most libations for poverty reduction World Bank 2004, Poverty Reduction Strategy Papers or Bangladesh, Nepal, Sri Lanka and Pakistan, Country Paper of India 2005]. Development research suggests that such factors tend to galvanize support for change and thus make the politics of policy reform easier for scoring higher on indicators related to the Millennium Development Goals (MDGs). Nevertheless, there is a widespread increase in a mismatch between policy reform and conditions of poverty, vulnerability and inequality, particularly that of rural women. The majority of states in south Asia have not been effective in giving operational value to their policy initiatives/changes and sectoral strategies. Hence, development policy's potential as a vehicle for fostering change in institutional norms and structures of poverty and inequality is undermined.

South Asian countries have an HDI value of 0584 and GDI value of 0535, which is 99 points lower than the average for developing countries [UN/HDR 2002]. This is exacerbated in most cases by unequal allocation of food, lower wage rates, and lack of inheritance rights of women [Ramakrishna and Rangacharyulu 1999]. Despite numerous cases of success in managing the village level governance and microfinance or self-help groups (SHGs), rural women of south Asia have significantly less access than men to livelihood resources, assets, health care, education, technology and community management.

The most extreme form of gender inequality is the fact that over 79 million women are "missing" in south Asia, largely due to familial neglect of girls, sex-selective abortions, social practices like dowry, property related murders, "honour killings", acid attacks and trafficking in women and girls [Human Development in South Asia, 2000].

Evidence from many countries in the region shows that disparities between women and men in their access to and control over resources are associated with women's systematically lower access to community governance, health and education facilities and less than optimal participation in economic decision-making [Elson 1991]. Existing materials point to the lower status of women throughout the region. The GDP per capita for women, for example, is extremely low and is often less than half, or one-third of that of men. In India it is 38 per cent; in Pakistan 30 per cent; in Sri Lanka 41 per cent; in Bhutan 51 per cent and in Bangladesh 58 per cent. The reason for the low GDP per capita for women and the reporting of women as economically less active (i e, in the range of 29 to 44 per cent in the above six countries) is determined by their low social status [Raju and Bagchi 1993]. Yet, when both household and "productive labour" for market considered, women work considerably longer hours than men do. This gap is particularly pronounced in poor households. The time that women allocate to agriculture or land-based labour is three to four times greater than that of their male partners [Mencher 1993]. However, customary practices throughout south Asia (with some exceptions in Sri Lanka and Bhutan) prevent women from exercising their right to own and control land. This results in their exclusion from the process of rural and agricultural development.

Women's movements, feminist researchers and numerous civil Society organizations in the region have expressed deep dissatisfaction over the current poverty assessments for failing to incorporate women's concerns or overlooking gender relations of inequality. Further more, community perceptions are given great weight in participatory assessments, but these reflect social norms and values that tend to overlook gender inequalities in resources, voice and women's vulnerability to violence and economic risks. Measures like Gender Development Index (GDI) and Gender Related Empowerment Measures (GEM) adopted to indicate the level of women's development have not been able to capture the position gained by women in accessing livelihoods. As a result, such indices have failed to grasp real achievements and also the barriers against rural women.

Poverty diagnostic data are rarely gender segregated and likewise is the case of data on the informal economy and macro-economic policies. The systems of national accounts in south Asia are seriously affected by statistical invisibility of women. There is poor conceptualization of women's economic roles and inadequate attention to home production, household work and unpaid family labour. Within these limits, this paper barely scratches the surface of this complex subject of development effectiveness through gender man streaming.

To describe women as silent observers of the male appropriation of power and resources oversimplifies both the women's voice if resistance and the range of ways in which they have addressed livelihoods. There are women who speak publicly about the continuing male dominance and control of livelihood resources. Of course, many women are silent but would speak if power and resource inequalities did not create obstacles. Some choose not to speak publicly but instead exercise informal resistance in what James Scott describes "off stage defiance" (1985, p. 23) and "infra politics of subordinate groups ... a wide variety of low profile forms of resistance that dare not speak in their own name" (1990, p. 19). There are also women who keep quiet and show nothing nut compliance to male dominance; this is done as a result of fear of insult and physical assault. Moreover, gender-based domination have typically been both personal and community-based; joint reproduction in the family and home without any control over productive resources has meant that "imagining an entirely separate existence for the women as a subordinated group requires a more radical step than it has for poor peasants, working class or slaves" [Scott 1990, p 19]. It against their oppression and subordination group, they may be socialized into accepting a view of their position and interest as prescribed from above, in maintaining patriarchal control within and outside their communities, or at least seek a space in "macroeconomic policies".

As noted above, development policy in macroeconomic analysis has shown some concern in bringing about limited change in formal institutions, while paying much less attention to informal institutions that govern day to day life, and working through informal constraints called codes of conduct or norms of behaviour. These form part of the tradition that we call culture and which affects women's sense of the possible. "For those at the high end of hierarchy, it provides the means to maintain their high position, whereas for those at the low end, it can limit aspirations, create discrimination and block mobility" [North of capital, p 170]. As Bourdieu argues, culture, therefore is a form of capital which makes it possible for certain individuals and groups (men in this case) to maintain and enhance their social, economic and political power. This type of social order plays an important role in the reproduction/perpetuation of gender inequality.

Gender equality is seen as only a goal, a social desirability to which many people think they should be seen to agree. Surely, that is a step forward in non-discrimination. But, south Asia still lacks a critical mass of people who are willing to launch public action for women's equality of access to livelihood opportunities (equality in employment/self-employment and control of property and assets) and equality of reward or pay in work.

Changes in Livelihoods: Women's Economic Activity Rate

In assessing changes in women's livelihoods in the last 10 years, we start with the overall position of women in the workforce and changes therein. One major problem that is faced in interpreting the available data is that the time series are often not comparable over time or between countries. Definitions are changed and this in turn makes it difficult to compare times series. For instance, the reference period or the reference age for labour force participation rates have changed, leading to major swings in data. But, at a broad level, women's labour force participation rates show women's economic participation in non-domestic work. An equivalent measure is women's economic activity rate: The share of the women population of ages 15 and above, who supply, or are available to supply labour for the production of goods and services [UNDP/HDR 2004, p. 269].

As a first approximation, this table shows that most countries of south Asia did not show much improvement, although none of them regressed in women's economic activity rates. There is a marked improvement in Pakistan, which, however, started at a much lower level of women's economic activity and this remains at 44 per cent, the lowest of all south Asian countries in comparison to men's economic activity rate.

Table 1: Women's Economic Activity Rate for South Asian Countries (Ages 15 and Above)

(As per cent of male rate)

Country	*Rate (per cent) 2002*	*Index (1990=100) 2002*	*As per cent of Male Rate*
Bangladesh	66.6	101	76
Bhutan	57.1	100	65
India	42.4	105	50
Maldives	65.4	100	80
Nepal	56.8	101	67
Pakistan	36.3	127	44
Sri Lanka	43.3	108	59

Source: UNDP, Human Development Report, 2004, Table 27, 'Gender Inequality in Economic Activity', pp. 229-32.

Table 2: Women's Status in Employment

(Per cent of total)

Country	*Wage/Salary workers*	*Own-Account workers*	*Contributing family workers*
Bangladesh			
1991	5.2	6.4	-
1996	8.7	7.8	77.3

2000	8.3	11	73.2
India			
1993-94	43.60	18.12	38.81
1999-2000	44.19	17.77	38.04
Pakistan			
1990	22.6	12.9	-
1995	24.8	13.5	61.7
2000	33.1	16.8	50.1

Note: We could not incorporate Maldives and Sri Lanka in this table and consequently in Table 3 due to lack of availability of comparable figures for these years.

Source: ILO, 2003, Key Indicators of the Labour Market, Table 'Status in Employment', for all countries, except India. NSS Rounds 1993-94 and 1999-2000, as calculated by Sandip Sarkar, Institute for Human Development, New Delhi, December 2004.

Table 3: Percentage Point Changes in Distribution of Women Workers by Status

Country	*Wage/Salary Earners*	*Own-Account Workers*	*Contributing Family workers*
Bangladesh	1996-2000	1996-2000	1996-2000
	-0.4	3.2	-4.1
India	1993-2000	1993-2000	1993-2000
	1.13	-0.35	-0.77
Pakistan	1995-2000	1995-2000	1995-2000
	8.3	3.3	-11.6

Source: Calculated from above.

Comparative levels are attained in Bangladesh and the Maldives, with 76 per cent and 80 per cent, respectively. What this shows is that: *(a)* progress in most of south Asia has been very slow or has only kept up with increases in the labour force; *(b)* there is a long way to go before they match the performance of southeast or east Asia, where for example, it is 85 per cent for Thailand and 86 per cent for China [UNDP 2004].

Concerning the economic activity rate, there is the question of women's status-as contributing family workers, own-account workers or wage and salary workers. A high proportion of women as contributing family workers will be accompanied by a long proportion of women as independent earners. Consequently, a reduction in the proportion of women contributing family workers may be taken as an improvement in their status as independent income earners.

There are numerous changes in the method of calculation of the above data, which make it difficult to make comparisons. Nevertheless, one broad conclusion is possible: There has been a movement of women away from "contributing family workers" towards both "wage and salary workers" and "own account workers" in most of south Asia, with only India showing almost no change in these proportions. This means that there is a movement in the direction of women being income earners away from being family workers. In Bangladesh there has been the development of the export-based readymade garments industry, which now absorbs about two million women as factory workers. In India, the movement out of family workers into income earners has been mainly into casual, home-based workers or "own account workers" in the above classification [Horton 1996].

Agricultural Workers

Few dispute that an overwhelming majority of the economically active in agriculture are women. In 1997, close to 70 per cent of the women of working age in low-income, food-deficit countries were engaged in agricultural work [IFAD 2002]. Yet women own less than 2 per cent of all land and receive only 5 per cent of extension services worldwide. *(ibid)*. In south Asia, approximately 3 to 10 per cent of rural women own land which they cultivate. Bina Agarwal (1994) has argued that land defines the social status and political power in the village. The exclusion of women from the allocation of intra household resources limits their power of control over land-based livelihoods. This is further reinforced by: *(a)* socio-cultural perceptions of physical and biological constraints on women's work; and *(b)* patriarchal property ownership practices where land/property is inherited from father to son (or another close male relative in the absence of son) in most of south Asia, with exceptions in Bhutan, partly in Maldives, and some pocket in north-east India like Khasi, Garo and Jaintia Hills. However, we have still not addressed the question whether women's lack of ownership and control of agricultural land affects productivity. Recently, the taskforce on Technological Empowerment if Women in Agricultural of National Commission for Women in India recommended that "women be recognized as cultivators in their own right. This would enable them to get loans and become active partners in the acquisition of farm equipment and management of their farm" [The Hindu, January 11, 2005]. The proportion of women's employment in south Asia (Table 4) shows that a large number of them are engaged in agriculture.

There is some structural change in rural women's sect oral workforce participation. There is very little movement out of agriculture. As Table 6 shows, there is increase in women's participation as agriculture in Maharashtra region in India [Parikh, Acharaya and Krishnaraj 2004] noted the increase in the number women's work in the capacity of laborers, while most of the cultivators are men; from 51.58 per cent (men 38.70 per cent) in 1991 to 54.22 per cent (men 41.63 per cent) in 2001. The 55th NSS round of 1999-2000 noted 57.70 per cent rural women engaged as agricultural labourers and men 45.60 per cent, in the same region. Although these women gain in incomes, it is relatively less as compared to men.

The daily agricultural wage of women was reported in the range of Rs 35-38, while that of men was Rs 45-50; with unemployment in the range of 8 to 10 per cent [NSS 55th round, as given in Parikh, Acharaya, Krishnaraj 2004].

Informal Work

Throughout south Asia, the informal workers have grown both in absolute and relative terms, to the formal sector workers [ILO 2003]. This growth can also be seen in terms of growing casualisation of the workforce. In India, women and men informal workers constituted about 72 and 68.4 per cent of the workforce respectively in the country. High proportion informal workers were found in trade, hotels and restaurants, followed by manufacturing [UNIFEM and SEWA Bharat 2002]. In Bangladesh between 1983-84 and 1995-96, the number of women among the informal workers increased from 44 per cent to 75 per cent, [Mahmud 2000]. Interestingly, the growth rate for male labor force during 1995-96 to 1999-2000 stands at 1.2 per cent, while for women this growth rate in the labour force during the same period is 14.4 per cent [Statistical Profile of Women in Bangladesh 2002: p. 137]. According to 1991 figures for Nepal, the majority of informal workers are women: 83.7 per cent women and 69.5 per cent men and they were self-employed [Human Development in South Asia 2000:60]. A study of Pakistan [Klein and Nestvogel 1999] reported that approximately 1, 00,000 women worked in brick kilns, but were not officially employed because, although the entire families worked, only the men were registered as the head of the households.

Women's entry into the workforce in south Asia has largely been in the informal economy. The UNIFEM-SEWA Bharat organized workshop in New Delhi in December 2002, noted three distinct outcomes of the current economic reforms and associated deregulation process: *(a)* growth of the informal sector; *(b)* greater feminization of labour market with widening gender wage differentials (women being paid far less than men for the same or similar work); *(c)* re-emergence of home-based work as an important constituent of industrial production.

Table 4: Employment of Women is South Asia by Major Sectors

(In per cent)

Country	*Agriculture*	*Industry*	*Service*
Bangladesh (1996)	41.7	27.8	30.5
India (1994)	78	10.9	11.1
Nepal (1996)	93.7	1.4	4.5

Pakistan (1997)	66.4	10.6	23.2
Sri Lanka (1995)	41.5	30.8	27.7

Source: Mahbuh ul Haq Development Centre, 2000, Table 4.2.

Workshop proceeding showed (p. 8) the unorganized sector (not considering agriculture) accounts for over 90 per cent of all women workers, including wageworkers, piece rate workers and the self-employed. The growing presence of women in the household industry of India showed a steady increase from 2.06 million in 1981 to 4.23 million in 1991 and to 8.08 million in 2001 (based on Census of India 2001).

Migration and Gender Inequality

In Asia as a whole there has been an increasing feminisation of migration, with women constituting 1.5 million or more than 16 per cent of total Asian migrant workers in 2000 [IOM 14]. Of total migrants, it is also estimated that 30 to 40 per cent are "irregular" migrants, who have no legal status and consequently no protection of their rights. One south Asian country in which women's migration is far greater than that of men is Sri Lanka. The proportion of women migrants has ranged from 95.2 per cent of the total in 1996 to 88.8 per cent in 2000 [IOM 22]. Most of them fall into the "housemaid" and "unskilled" categories.

Women migrate for livelihood needs to support themselves and their families. In the process women are able to emerge as independent income earners. While this is a benefit to women, it comes at a cost. Often the women who migrate as maids themselves have families and children. While they go to earn an income through looking after other people's families and children, they face the alienation of not being able to look after their own families and children. In addition to migration for meeting the household's basic needs for food, shelter and economic security, the needs or motivations for women to migrate include: *(a)* "elements of society that limit a woman's personal development, marriage with dowry, etc"; and *(b)* "escape from vorced, widowed, etc" [IOM 2003].

The importance of migration can be seen in the role of remittances by migrant workers. It is the largest or second-largest source of foreign exchange in a number of south Asian countries, including India, Sri Lanka, Bangladesh and Pakistan. World-wide remittances from migrant workers are greater than ODA and private capital flows to developing countries put together. In 2000, India ranked first in the world for remittances, while Bangladesh ranked eighth in the world. Migrant women play and important role in the economic development of both the migrant and immigrant countries through financial contributions from remittances, the improvement of their own skills and education; and also influence the societies of origin by spreading new norms of mobility and values about women's rights and opportunities.

Increasing Development Effectiveness

In the new conceptualisation of poverty reduction, access livelihood resources, capabilities building, security against vulnerability and equality of gender have come to be viewed as one integral process of the national plans of macroeconomic and social policies to promote growth and reduce poverty [The World

Bank's Annual Review of Development Effectiveness (2004); Attacking Poverty (2000-01)]. Engendering Development (2001) and the work of scholars such as Amartya Sen (1993) identify the following dimensions of poverty: *(a)* lack of access to labour markets and employment opportunities and productive resources; *(b)* lack of access to capabilities and public services as education and health; *(c)* vulnerability to economic risks and to public and domestic violence, as well as constrains on mobility; *(d)* lack of representation/empowerment, being without voice and without power at the household, community and national/international levels. It is further argued that development assistance has not done enough to dismantle patriarchal structures of power and to change women's gender identity of subordination both in productive and reproductive roles. Despite numerous cases of success in managing the village level governance and microfinance groups, rural women of south Asia still have significantly less access than men to resources, assets, services, knowledge, technology and community decision-making.

The term "gender mainstreaming" emerged in the early 1980s, as a concern of the international women's movement for alternative strategies to move women's issues out of the periphery and into the "mainstream" of development decision-making. In the years following the Beijing Conference in 1995, gender mainstreaming has been referred to as a comprehensive strategy that involves the integration of women-oriented programmes and gender issues into development institutions. Gender mainstreaming is a process to achieve gender equality and overcome the costs of women's marginalization. Mainstreaming requires:

(a) incorporation of gender concerns in planning, policy and implementation to provide effective rights and dignity to the disadvantaged, *(b)* ending domestic and public violence, *(c)* recognition of women's work (productive and reproductive) and contribution to economy as well as their economic agency.

Unequal gender relations affect the way in which the burden of poverty is distributed, and unequal gender relations can also be the cause of poverty among women and girls in otherwise non-poor families. Thus unequal gender relations need to be addressed both as a cause and as a factor in the intensification of poverty.

Women's Agency and Well-being

Women's agency defined as the capacity for autonomous action in the face of constricting social sanctions and structural inequalities. This, in turn, offers a frame work in which constraint is seen as constitutive of gender norms and relations between women and men, which are entrenched and durable but not unchanging. Enhancing women's agency requires action on a number of fronts. Poverty rights, access to finance including microfinance, building of women's organisations, effective participation in community forums, measures to curb domestic and public violence on women, tackling discrimination against the girl child in matters of nutrition, health care and education—all these aspects of transforming gender relations [IFAD 2002]. Studies on Microcredit in Bangladesh have shown that this does happen when women become income earners; they are able to use more of household income to improve their own well-being, thus reducing poverty within households. It further improves women's mobility, social visibility, dignity and self-esteem [Kelkar, Nathan, Jahan 2004]. The basis of this strategylies in the recognition if sine crucial interrelations between reducing gender inequality and reducing poverty.

- Since women experience greater poverty than men, it is necessary that women be enabled to improve their own well-being.
- There is substantial evidence to show that women's empowerment, or agency enhancement, can benefit not only women themselves but also children and men.
- Women's education, economic independence, increase in remunerative employment, political mobilisation and so on, altogether have a substantial effect in reducing the number of births, and also reduce child mortality rates for both girls and boys.
- Women's active participation in community management and control over productive assets can increase the efficiency with which households and communities can use their human, natural and other resources.
- Environmental regeneration requires both the active participation of women as community managers, and their increased economic participation in order to transform natural resource use patterns.
- Women's agency can have an impact on society as a whole through raising issues of social transformation.

Over the last decade, there has been a slow, partial and even fitful change in women's education, their representation in governance and their status as independent an advance for women? their own right. But is such a movement an advance for women? Does it represent a capability development, an increase in their own well-being, and in their freedom of choice? Has it weakened the grip of patriarchy or does it function within the confines of traditional relations?

We look at these questions taking two major sites of this transformation—first, women as wage workers in the garment industry in Bangladesh and second, women as own-account producers in the informal economy. In both cases, whether as wage workers or own account producers, there is the role of women as income earners, one which is different from their former and traditional status as dependent family workers. There is the increase in dignity that goes along with being a wage earner, often even the major income provider in the family. This is different from women's work in family agriculture; women's contribution would have been subsumed in the general household labour and not even acknowledged as productive labour, given that men are generally the owners of land in south Asia.

Women's earnings from wage labour in garment manufacture, although low, were still twice of what they could have earned in the formal economy or in rural areas [World Bank 1995: 73]. It was further found that 57 per cent of women garment workers determined how their own wages are spent and also that their husbands contributed 1.3 to 3.7 hours of household work per day [World Bank 1995: 75].

With both wage labour and own-account production, women have greater prestige in the family and also have a greater control over how their incomes is spent, which is what Amartya Sen's (1990) theory of household bargaining as cooperative conflict would predict. Women are able to direct more or the household income towards their own and their children's well-being and even control or reduce wasteful consumption, as in the case of alcohol consumption by men among Chenchu in Andhra Pradesh, India [Nathan, Kelkar 2004].

At the same time, this advance should not blind us to the inadequacies in the new forms of women's incorporation in global chains. The advance is fitful, as in most of south Asia. Further, as the Asian crisis showed in east and southeast Asia, there can be reversals of this movement, with market downturns forcing women back into household and domestic roles as they perform the role of shock absorbers to macro-economic downturns [Nathan and Kelkar, 1999]. The uncertainties and risks of own-account workers, low wages and sexual harassment for those in the workplace, all associated with the new ways of women's incorporation in global chains are only aspects of the lack of what the ILO calls decent work " it involves opportunities for work that is productive and delivers a fair income, security in the workplace and social protection for families, better prospects for personal development and social integration, freedom for people to express their concerns, organize and participate in the decisions that effect their lives and equality of opportunity and treatment for all women and men [ILO,www.ilo.org/public/English/decent.

In advancing the struggle of women workers for decent work, some major issues need to be confronted. First is that the gender differentiation of the labour force between a core of men who have somewhat decent work standards and a flexible mass of women workers who do not have these standards, largely proceeds on the basis of skill. Women are kept out of skilled categories or their labour, even though skilled, is classified as unskilled. This skill-based gender differentiation of the labour force needs to be confronted and changed, if the conditions of women workers are to change.

Impact on Household Well-being

Perhaps because of women's gender responsibility of provisioning the household (acquiring and processing food) women tend to spend more of the income they control for household consumption goods. This is in contrast to the behaviour of men who tend to spend more of the income they control, on themselves, alcohol entertainment, etc, and consequently neglect the consumption needs of children and others in the household.

What this shows is that the well-being or poverty-reducing impact of an increase in household income is greater when the increased income is controlled by women than when it is controlled by men. The poverty-reducing impact of development interventions increases when women's agency is enhanced within the household.

Studies by Dreze and Sen (2002) and Deolalikar (2005) show a clear correlation between women's educational status and infant and child mortality. This probably works in two ways. On the one hand, women are able use the knowledge they acquire from education (and mobility, we should add). On the other hand, women's education is likely to increase their role in household decision-making. Both of these routes together lead to an improvement in infant and child nutrition states. "Many empirical studies from around suggest that the gender disparities in health, schooling and nutritional outcomes of children tend to narrow with mother's schooling, as mother (relative to fathers) tend to invest more in their female children" [Deolalikar 2005: 112].

Land and Efficiency of Resource Use

An increasing range of econometrically robust studies shows that land and asset ownership by women have significantly better outcomes for their agency as well as for child survival, education and health, than those owned only by men [for discussion see Agarwal 1994, Kelkar 1992, National Commission on Farmers Report 2004].

Not being landowners is at least part of the reason why women are not perceived as "farmers" even when they do much of the farm work. As a result, agricultural extension and information on new technologies are almost exclusively directed to men, even when women are traditionally responsible. Although vegetable cultivation in almost universally women's work, projects that aim to diversify agricultural production by promoting commercial vegetable cultivation (as in Bangladesh) often train, or used to train, the men. Something is "inevitably" lost when the knowledge is "passed on" to women. If women wee accepted would be targeted for training as farm managers, and not only as home managers.

In the midst of increasing feminization of agriculture, women lack title to land which is one of the causes for the persistent gender inequality. A recent analysis of state of Indian farmers by the National Commission on Farmers (NCF) emphasizes that lack of title to land makes it difficult for women farmers to access institutional credit. "For example, hardly 5 per cent of women seem to have been issued with kissan credit cards out of the many millions to whom such cards have been issued.... Extension and input supply services also do not reach women at the right time and place. Therefore, as stressed by the NCF, there is need for a new deal for women in agriculture" [M.S. Swaminathan, 'The Sons of the Soil', *The Hindu*, April 19, 2005].

Thus, new deal for women in agriculture, along with necessary inputs and credit support could increase the efficiency of resource use and thus contribute to increasing production. This is borne out by an ongoing IFAD project in Bangladesh, the Aquaculture Development Project. In this project women were exclusively trained in fish aquaculture and provided credit for commercial fish culture in ponds owned by their men. With this knowledge and credit women were able to transform pond aquaculture from a semi-subsistence mode to a regular commercial mode, with an increase in productivity of more than 50 per cent [Nathan and Jahan 2004]. Women in Andhra Pradesh, India also used microcredit to take on lease, lands that were being fitfully cultivated and develop them into regular cultivation with higher productivity than earlier.

Transforming the management and ownership status of household resources can help increase productivity particularly were these resources are underutilized. In Pakistan and Nepal, large migration of men has left women as de facto farm managers. But there management decisions are constrained by their inability to access credit on time—as the land remains in the names of men, and their signatures are needed before credit can be given. There are consequent losses due to failure to procure and use inputs on time.

An overall review of forest regeneration movements [Kelkar and Nathan, 2003] showed both that management and regeneration suffered and conversely that when women were mobilized there was a greater impact on forest cover and environmental regeneration. Collection of fuel from forest lands was the last part of the household labour to be intensified and that it resulted from the very low opportunity cost of women's labour which resulted in the overuse of women's labour and the wood fuel that was produced with that labour [Nathan and Kelkar, 1997]. More detailed analysis [Kelkar and Nathan, 2005] of the connections between gender equality and fuel consumption patterns brought out the proposition that the low opportunity cost of women's labour limits the adoption of improved stoves and that women's entry into income-earning activities would promote fuel transition.

Microfinance and Change in Gender Relations

Major advances in women's livelihood condition have been through the institution of microfinance and their participation in the local markers. Starting in Bangladesh, through the innovations of Grameen Bank and BRAC, microfinance institutions (MFIs), whether in the form of NGO-run credit groups or the Indian variety of self-help groups (SHGs), have now become a ubiquitous feature of women's livelihood programmes. Microfinance in India covers over 11.6 million poor households accessing banking services through their 0.77 million SHGs and the SHG-Bank Linkage programme is reported to be the largest in the world in terms of its outreach [IFAD 2004:64]. In Bangladesh, they have promoted women's entry into income earning occupations and have had an impact on women's empowerment [see Kabeer 2001 and Kelkar, Nathan and Jahan 2004 for analysis of women's empowerment through MFIs in Bangladesh].

The rise of women's micro-enterprises, poultry rearing, vegetable growing, and so on, his made women's income a permanent component of household income and weakened the "purdah" relationship of the secluded women dependent of the male provider. Further the incomes earned from microcredit financed activities of women are not just temporary or irregular. They have become an integral part of the household budget. The household's living standard, whatever it might be, depends in part at least, on this stream of income continuing. Thus, there is a change in the picture of men being the breadwinners; which is one part of the gender relations of purdah. The change in one part of this relation of purdah, that of dependence, cannot but have impacts on the other part of the relationship, that of women's seclusion, consequently weakening the position of purdah as a sigh of the woman's or household's social standing.

The weakening of seclusion itself has been noticed in a number of ways—women's greater presence in the market as buyers, though only very restricted as sellers; women's participation in various types of agricultural fieldwork; women's unescorted movement, though often in a group and not alone, to the marker, to schools, to attend training, and so on.

A weakness of the change studied is that, by and large, there is still the expectation that women are solely responsible for domestic labour and for maintaining the rhythm of family life. We noted a few instances of men taking up some domestic responsibilities, particularly when women are away on training, or doing some subsidiary domestic work, like cleaning food for cooking, though not taking responsibility. But these are still very few instances. More widespread as the acceptance of some disruption of family life, such as meals being late when there is a meeting. But, overall, it is still true that women are almost entirely responsible for domestic work, which means that the price they have to pay foe some improved well-being, and increased self-respect and influence in households matters is that of increasing their hours of work. The commercialisation of formerly domestic and labour–consuming tasks, like dehusking, has helped women reduced some work burdens. Nevertheless, the price women have to pay for their successes is that of working longer hours. This is no doubt a critical weakness of the change in gender relations that poor, rural women are going through, a weakness that will continue until the conjunction of domestic with other, productive labour is challenged.

Importantly, some men are beginning to realize the opportunity cost of women's labour and this makes them ready to share some of the "domestic" tasks, like fetching water, drying paddy and taking care of children. Interestingly, women view this as the only way of dealing with the constraint/overload of productive and reproductive work.

Women's Transformational Role

These are many examples, from many parts of the world, of the transformational role of women. The struggles of Argentinean and other Latin American women (Mothers against the Disappeared ones) were instrumental in securing widespread human rights for their societies as a whole. The activities of the self-Employed Women's Association (SEWA) and the Working women's Forum (WWF) in India, the Grameen Bank in Bangladesh and many other women-centred NGOs have brought to centrestage the role of the informal sector and of women's contribution to economic development. They have transformed the definitions of "employment" and "trade union" and initiated many regulations that have improved the conditions of work and life. Strategic gender impact and women's social transformational roles have also been observed in many IFAD and UNIFEM funded projects in Asia, for example:

- In the Andhra Pradesh Tribal Development Project, self-help groups of women took up contracts for local construction and, with the help of supportive bureaucrats, were instrumental in the elimination of contractors for such works in all indigenous peoples' areas of the state. More recently, federations of SHGs in the project have taken on multiple functions in addressing social and administrative issues at the block and sub divisional levels. They have taken up issues like construction of toilets, repairs of roads, improvements in drinking water and electricity supply—all matters of good governance at the local level.

- Such matters of good governance were also taken up by well established women's SHGs in Maharashtra—insisting on proper provision of social services, like drinking water and bus services, like drinking water and bus services.
- Women's individual access to productive resources, directly and not mediated by men, has been most successfully addressed in microfinance schemes, but rarely touched in other areas, particularly land and common resources, like forests and water. Rural women in significant numbers have bought or based agricultural land in their independent names in four districts in Bangladesh. The Aquaculture Development Project in Bangladesh is now trying to formulate measures to transfer effective control of household ponds to women.
- Gender discrimination is deeply embedded and reinforced by social and cultural system. To overcome these constraints projects like Dir and northern areas in Pakistan, East Java in

Indonesia, several projects in Bangladesh, and the Mewat project in Haryana, India will have to be innovative and negotiate with local religious leaders and scholars in order to get support to form women's organisations.

- In some cases, women have been able to move out of "a culture of apathy" [Douglas, 2004]. They now aspire to change themselves, their men and most of all their children. As confirmed by women, men and children in the Chenchu villages of Andhra Pradesh, India, there was substantial reduction in the drunkenness of men and violence within the home. Women emphasized that prior to Sangam (SHGs), "we were socially considered ignorant beings; we did not know how to carry ourselves and where a bus was going, now we know about the bus and Men are listening to us now. Our social prestige/respect in the community has improved because of our outside work, increased income, work in sangams, dealing with outsiders like the bank officers, the GCC staff, traders etc. People from the neighboring villages admire us for our work and ability to do these things. Men no longer order us to do things and where to go and not to go. Now we have acquired a social visibility and self-respect as women" [Nathan and Kelkar, 2004].
- Dealing with project and other officials on somewhat more equal terms, negotiating the intricacies of running the procurement centres, learning to keep accounts, learning to deal with the market and officials, and with their own

men, has not only led to material benefits in improved well-being, but it has also increased these women's agency and "capacity to aspire" [Appadurai, 2004]. This development of their "capacity to aspire" is the biggest guarantee that the achievements of the project will be sustained as women of Chenchu dare to take bigger strides for themselves and their families.

Women's Political Effectiveness

There is persistent belief that inclusion of women into the political process or governance would change the way in which the politics of development is carried out. That women are supposed to be more concerned about the common good: their style of development would be less corrupt and more cooperative. There are hardly any regional or national studies carried on the subject. A macro picture based on case studies suggests that a well-established "feature of institutionalized corruption makes it also rather unrealistic to expect women to be more clean politicians then men. Corruption in PRI [Panchayat Raj Institutions] is apparently a well-oiled machinery. In such circumstances, a representative would need a lot of resources, material as well as immaterial, to fight corruption and women are even more unlikely to have command over such resources" [Hust 2004: 199].

Evelin Hust further raises an important question in the countryside of Orissa (I would add south Asia), everybody is complaining about corruption, and women with their one-third representation and resource-poor conditions within the home and outside, are expected to carry out the heavy burden of ending corruption. This is an "overly idealistic hope" [Hust 2004: 200] and should not be put solely on the shoulders of women. This has resulted in silencing, even ousting many women leaders (sarpanchs) by the male patriarchs of the village. Ending corruption, like ending violence, is a task for the entire system of macro-governance and community management.

In spite of numerous obstacles to women's local political effectiveness, there is evidence, around south Asia that women members and leaders in the local governance do manage to articulate their perspectives in matters such as land transfers to women, education, water supply issues, roads, fuel, health care and toilets for women in Dalit areas [UNRISD 2005].

Women may have low political efficacy because of their inadequacy in proportional representation and poor endowment inadequacy in proportional representation and poor endowment in resources. Yet, all the available data indicates that in the local governance where women have effective presence, they are grounded in claims of gender strategic identity and seek to eliminate the subordination and discrimination stemming from patriarchal structures of power.

Ending Gender-based Violence

In a recently held World Conference on Women Beijing Plus 10, civil society groups expressed concern at the incidents of violence against women. That as long as there is gender-based violence, it is difficult to claim progress in human development. Gender equality requires protection from gender-based violence in domestic and public spaces, "Violence and aggression against women in public is seen as linked to the rise of conservative forces in society that aggressively and consciously act to prevent women's public appearances and participation" [Shaheed and Zaidi 2005, 14].

There are two inter-related project-specific questions of violence: *(a)* Do projects reduce violence over time? *(b)* How to deal with violence that comes up in implementing project activities? There are, for instance, reports that the organization of women into savings and credit groups or self-help groups has led to incidents of violence by men of their households; The violence was reportedly because of failure of women to perform their set household duties, like serving food to men on time. But in one way or the other such violence reflects a reluctance of men to come to terms with the changes in women's social visibility and in gender relations that tend to come about with changes in women's income status. At the same time, there are also reports that such violence tends to go down as the functioning of these women's groups gets established and as the importance of their economic contributions to the households are realized and accepted by men.

In recent studies in India and select countries, the costs of violence have been estimated to include economic loss experienced by the individual (like absence from paid work and/or lost productivity, expenses related to physical and mental health, lost lifetime earnings etc), the government through its health and social sector, the criminal justice system and employer and third party. The India study showed "that domestic violence can push economically fragile households into an economic crisis" (quoted in ISST, 2005: 43). An earlier study in India [UNIFEM 2003] estimated that women lost, on average, five working days after an incident of violence.

Violence against women has also personal and social effects: reduced quality of life, reduced mobility and participation in democratic process, and the effect on children. Public health workers in India reported women are afraid to travel alone outside the village for fear of being raped, thus limiting women's freedom and preventing them from participating in community and income-earning activities.

Building a coalition against violence is not usually seen as part of project activities in a poverty-reduction programme. But as has been argued in many places, violence against women is a development question, it is a question affecting women's agency. Building a coalition against such violence is necessary to addressing the strategic interests of women and to enhance their economic agency.

2

Rights of Women's on Land and Assets

The objective of this paper is to assess progress towards gender equality and rural poverty reduction through women's control over land and other productive resources, based on the experiences in some south Asian countries, namely, Bangladesh, India and Nepal. After briefly setting out a framework for understanding access to assets in the current context of structural reforms, the paper identifies a few key policy options in terms of mainstreaming gender in development programmes to achieve the Millennium Development Goals (MDGs).

While globally there has been a push for women's property and inheritance rights following the UN Convention on Elimination of All Forms of Discrimination against Women (CEDAW) commitment to equal access to land and other property (Articles 14, 15 and 16) in 1979, progress has been slow. In most of south Asia, women do have legal rights guaranteed by the constitution, yet they usually do not exercise them. In India and Sri Lanka, noninterference policies have been cited in relation to certain minority communities and indigenous peoples [FAO et al 2004:8]. Personal laws are invoked to counteract legal provisions.

There have been several reasons for this lack of action and implementation of property rights for women. Land inheritance, the major form of land acquisition in south Asia, is a key element of family and kinship relations, and a way of structuring social relations on the ground [Dube 1997]. Land is valued not just for material reasons or as a productive resource, but also for symbolic reasons in terms of identity, status and hierarchy within a given social context. Policies therefore do not enter a social vacuum, but rather influence the economic and social life of the household, and in this process, conflicts cannot be ruled out [Gupta 1997]. Women in south Asia are dependent on men for at least one key agricultural activity—ploughing—and also for security and social support, given the fragile nature of state-led social protection. Most women do have access and use rights to land though these are contingent on their relationships to men and unless the relationship breaks down, they often do not find a need to claim independent rights.

It is often assumed that poverty reduction would lead to gender equality. Research on sex ratios in India, however, point to the opposite, namely, that increasing prosperity can have perverse gender effects [Agnihotri 2000; Rustagi 2000]. It is therefore important to make a conceptual distinction between projects that seek to reduce poverty and enhance productivity and those that seek to empower women, as the strategies adopted could be different. Effective poverty targeting can ensure that short-term, material benefits reach the poorest without necessarily leading to enhanced voice and equality, as revealed by the review of several projects in this paper.

Structural Reform and Changing Livelihood Patterns

Most of south Asia has adopted some form of structural adjustment in the 1980s and 1990s, directed by IMF-World Bank packages. The objectives have been short-term stabilisation and long-term growth by reorienting production towards the market system and cutting back on state subsidies and interventions that encourage "market distortions". The implications for agriculture and the rural sector, which support more than 70 per cent of the population in most of these countries, have however been far from positive. In three of them—India, Nepal and Pakistan—there has been a slow down in agricultural growth over the 1990s in the table.

In Nepal, the Agriculture Perspective Plan (APP) launched in 1996, underscored the need to prioritise agriculture in the growth process. To accelerate growth, APP proposed substantial increases in investments in irrigation, rural roads, fertilizer and

Table 1: Growth Rates in Different Sectors

Country	*Agriculture*		*Industry*		*Services*	
	1980-81 to 1989-90	*1990-91 to 1997-98*	*1981-82 to 1990-91*	*1991-92 to 1998-99*	*1980-81 to 1989-90*	*1990-91 to 1999-00*
India	2.85	1.41	7.8	5.8	-	-
Pakistan	5.4	4.4	8.2	4.8	6.7	4.6
Bangladesh	2.29	3.29	3.64	3.89	6.06	6.44

Nepal	3.59	2.57	7.8	7.2	3.6	6.2
Sri Lanka	2.4	2.4	4.2	7.2	5.3	5.73

Source: Compiled from Human Development in South Asia 2001, Haq 2002 technology.

However, ignoring the APP, both input and output markets in agriculture were deregulated, price subsidies in fertilizers and capital subsidies in shallow tube wells abolished and subsidized credit withdrawn, leading to the collapse of the agricultural sector, dominated by small and marginal farmers. The share of agriculture in total output has declined, and benefits of reforms seem primarily to have gone to the urban business community [UNDP 2004:37]. The emphasis on free trade has adversely affected the poor, in the absence of institutions to safeguard their interests.

India and Pakistan have had similar experiences. While structural reforms have been slower in agriculture than other sectors, since the mid-1990s, India has gradually opened up its agricultural sector to international trade, signing the Uruguay Round Agreement (URA) of the General Agreement on Trade and Tariffs (GATT) in 1994. Some of the key fallouts have been falling extension services, less institutional credit and inadequate price support systems on the one hand and an increase in corporate agriculture on the other. Alongside a decline in the average annual growth rate of the agriculture [GoI 2002:22], real incomes, especially for small and marginal farmers, have eroded. For the first time, the poorest are facing a decline in annual cereal availability to the extent of 10kg per head between 1995-96 and 2000-01 (156.6 kg to 147.3 kg per capita) [Patnaik 2002:138]. The connection between public expenditure and poverty levels may not be straightforward, yet clearly, despite all charges of corruption or inefficiency, the state has a role to play in addressing issues of equality.

The withdrawal of the state is closely linked to a dependence on money and markets—the new themes within development discourse [Zwarteveen 1998]. This emphasis has had two types of implications: first treating assets such as land and water primarily as economic goods (hence justifying a range of user fees and contributions), and second, devolution of management control to overcome state in efficiencies as well as enhance incentives for more intensive resource utilization at the local level. While both these aspects, that is, local control and engagement with markets, offer potential opportunities to women, participation nevertheless involves challenging the status quo, overcoming a range of socio-economic barriers, and implies the existence of considerable social risk and uncertainty.Women's strategies thus often involve the use of more indirect means to obtain access to resources, be it land, water or trees. It is in recognition of this social embeddedness of productive resources, that many organisations working on the ground have in fact focused either on "creating new assets" for women in wastelands and other common property rather than claiming property rights over existing resources especially land, or organizing women into groups to better enable them to face risks.

Given the reality of both policy framework and the nature of markets, one needs to carefully examine the types of assets that can contribute to gender equality and women's empowerment.

Defining Assets

In 1995, out of 1.3 billion of the world's poor, 515 million lived in south Asia, and during the 1990s, the incidence of poverty increased in Pakistan, Bangladesh and Sri Lanka [Haq 2002:48]. While a majority of the population of south Asia resides in rural areas and is primarily dependent on agriculture, one not only finds a decline in per capita cultivable land over the last two decades, but also a growing disparity in the pattern of landownership. In Bangladesh, for instance, 50 per cent of rural households are functionally landless (<0.2 ha) [Hossain et al 2000], in India close to 60 per cent have less than 0.40 hectares (56 per cent of male headed and 75 per cent of female headed households) (NSS data) and in Nepal while 29 per cent are landless, another 47 per cent own less than 0.5 hectares of land [UNDP 2004]. The pattern of landownership reveals both caste and gender disparities, with women owing about 10 per cent of the land, but the size of these holdings being on average two-thirds that of men.

States have tried to implement some form of land reform programme post-independence, despite the fact that the quantum of such land available for distribution is nominal. Bangladesh for instance has 2.1 million ha of government-controlled surplus ("khas") land, and even if equally distributed to the 10.5 million landless households, each would get less than 0.5 acres, not considered viable as an insurance mechanism [Khan 2004:85]. Yet as Barkat et al (2001) demonstrate, less than 50 per cent has been distributed and of this, less than half to the landless. Amongst the genuine people who got listed and land allocated to them, more than half (56 per cent) could not retain it due to physical threats, false deeds, corruption and so on, Instances of successful claims to land can be found where the landless beneficiaries have organised themselves and struggled to retain control over the land, with assistance from trade unions, NGOs and other civil society actors, but also where support in terms of credit, inputs marketing and price-support has been forthcoming (ibid: 155). In such a context, for women to claim rights to land appears even more problematic.

Data from all over south Asia not surprisingly then reveals that the share of agriculture to household incomes has been declining over the past decade, landownership is no longer the predominant source of household income in rural areas, and more and more rural people have been driven to look for alternate incomes and employment sources, largely in the urban, informal sector, in trade and services. As Heyer (1989) found in her Tamil Nadu study, asset strategies of the landless involved investing in human resources such as education and in social support networks, rather the land.

Most of the non-farm income is constituted of male income as women's literacy status has disadvantaged them in the labour markets. Studies reveal that while women, may be employed for more number of days, this is at the lowest level of informal employment, where the work is piece-rate and lower paid. There is hence a decline in their net earnings. It is only in Sri Lanka that women's labour force participation has been steadily increasing in all sectors in the 1990s at a faster rate than for men [CENWOR 1998]. This growing visibility of women, while not fully taken into account in state-run projects and programmes including land distribution and skill development, has led to an increase in domestic violence at the household level, with husbands feeling frustrated about losing a part of their "provider" role.

It is interesting to note that educated rural women are not just better able to secure formal employment than men [Harriss-White and Janakarajan 2004], but their aspirations too change and they are resistant to undertaking agricultural work, except in managerial-supervisory roles [Ramakumar 2003]. The first report of the National Commission on Farmers [GoI 2004: xiii] confirms the need to rethink the concept of "work" for rural women to include not just hard, manual labour, but also a range of other community activities such as preparation of noon meals, running of crèches and day care centres. Education and skills seem to be contributing to differentiation, rather than just landholdings, hence it is important to enable women to compete in these areas.

Within the livelihoods approaches, assets have been defined as a set of "capitals" that include natural, physical, human, social and financial capitals, all of which jointly play a key role not just in poverty reduction, but also in reducing vulnerabilities to stressed and shocks [Scoones 1998]. If one adopts a livelihoods approach, it would be important to explore the plethora of resources available in a given context—who has access to and control over what resource and the implications of this for gender equality. Apart from land, in the rural context, one could then considered livestock and labour as key individual/household assets, and common property, whether forest, grazing land or water resources (including marine and coastal) as community/state assets. For women particularly, public infrastructure supports in the form of drinking water, electricity and health facility are major assets, as they directly reduce their burden of work. In this context, the identification of reduction of time poverty for women and girls by the MDG Task Force Report as a strategy for gender equality is welcome [Birdsall et al 2004].

All rural livelihoods involve domestic labour to maintain and reproduce the household over time. Women play a central role in providing these services: child care, food preparation, fuel and water collection, care of the ill and elderly, and a range of activities that move into food production and income generating work, such as livestock care, homestead gardening and so on. Livelihood research pays lip-service to these activities and there are still too few studies that routinely collect data on domestic work alongside descriptions and analysis of occupations, employment and farm production [Jackson and Rao 2004], or provide them equal recognition as legitimate forms of work. A few that exist such as by Sarin (1997) note that the closure of forest for protection by community-based Joint Forest Management groups (JFM is a widespread programme within rural India) has led to firewood collections now involving greater time and longer journeys to more distant forests by women. This is also a finding in Agarwal's (1997) study of JFM in eight Indian states. Yet, a study Nepal by Cooke (2000) found that while women still spend more time than men in collection, the increased collection time comes almost equally from women and men.

Assets then can be meaningfully understood as offering a range of "entitlements": ownership (through trade, production, own-labour or inheritance); exchange (through market-based trade or transfers from the state, such as public works, social security and food subsides) and legal [Sen 1981]. Poverty rights particularly are fuzzy and mediated by family and kinship ties, and a strict focus on legal rights, can jeopardize women's rights to land, often unrecorded. The difficulties posed for women due to the legal framework of individual titling followed in most developing countries has in fact led to a rethinking of this strategy at the global level, with a shift towards more locally negotiated rights [World Bank 2001].

An "entitlements": approach is at its core a political struggle over negotiating power relations, whether through legal recognition or manipulation of custom. In the case of land, this would imply recognition of inheritance rights, but also other "secondary" rights. What is needed then is to strengthen women's bargaining power and control over decision-making, not just through legal entitlements over physical assets, which is one crucial aspect, but also by strengthening other sources of entitlements, as different assets may have different meanings for men and women, and these too could vary with context. While land is a major physical asset for most rural communities, it may become a non-asset if its productive use is restricted. In the war zones of Sri Lanka, for instance, rather than investing in land, households tend to invest in easily moveable items, such as jewellery [Korf 2004:289], take to migration and so on. It is only when access to and control over all the different assets or "capitals" collapse, that women or for that matter households, are unable to cope with vulnerability and move towards destitution.

If one looks at resource rights as a range of entitlements, with different routes to access (inheritance, markets, user groups, state transfers, etc.) and control, a helpful framework for discussion of gender equality, is one development by Sara Long we. She sees empowerment as a process that moves through five levels of equality, from welfare and access through conscientisation to participation and control. The level of control within this framework denotes a control over decision-making processes at par with men. This is important in the case of land, which is rarely considered individual property by either men or women, but seen as a joint household resource, whose use is subject/open to negotiation. Women do not act as autonomous individuals in relation to land, but neither do men, as both have gendered roles to play and gendered ideologies to live up to. Hence demanding a legal title that threatens the symbolic elements of landownership and the relationships these represent, is likely to be both resented and resisted. The problem for women arises when the marriage breaks down, and lacking a legal title, they are then threatened with destitution.

A second important point is clearly the complementarity between assets—land, livestock and labour – that tend to mutually reinforce each other. This also points to the possibilities of different staring points, rather than a single blueprint for south Asia. While group approaches for women in terms of joint land use may be problematic due to caste–class intersections apart from gender differences, new institutional approaches for control of equipment and inputs, infrastructure (such as irrigation), enhancing the level of skills to engage in new forms of production, may lead to improved gender equality outcomes. The key implication of such an understanding would be to create an enabling environment for control over a range of livelihood assets on the one hand, while also ensuring women's voices and rights in the new institutions being created to manage common resources.

Violence and Intra-household Disparities: A Result of Assetlessness

There is considerable evidence to show that the lack of assets enhances vulnerability and also poverty in its larger sense, but in addition, assetless women are subject to threats of violence and allocational inequalities within the household. While the lack of productive assets puts women at a structural disadvantage and can thus be seen to contribute to violence, the threat of violence itself inhibits participation, and economic vulnerability is a major reason for women's acceptance of it in their daily lives [Lloyd and Taluc 1999]. There is at the same time considerable evidence of violence against women who are making claims to property rights, an extreme example being that of branding and killing women as witches [Kelkar and Nathan 1991].

Based on a study of 500 households in Kerala, Panda [2003:34-35] notes that more than 35 per cent of women reported experiencing either physical or psychological violence within their marriage. This is despite the fact that Kerala has high levels of women's literacy, favourable sex rations and a generally enabling environment for women. The regression analysis to identify major causal factors finds a strong negative correlation between property ownership, and violence, followed by the husband's employment status. Even if a women does not use the exit option, the very existence of immovable property in her name could deter the husband from violence [Panda and Agarwal 2005:824]. A similar correlation can be assumed in the context of HIV. If women have a secure home, a site for economic activity and collateral for credit, they could potentially reduce risk factors (violence, risky behaviour) and if infected, can better cover costs and cope with the infection [Strickland 2004:11-12].

There have been several studies on intra-household allocation of roles, responsibilities and resources in south Asia. Yet these are not fixed, but change as a result of external factors, be it macro-policy shifts or micro-project interventions. Akram-Lodhi's (1996:97) analysis of time allocation data by class and gender across activities based on the baseline survey of the Salinity Control and Reclamation Project (SCARP) of Mardan in the North West Frontier Province, funded by the World Bank, CIDA and government of Pakistan, reveals that while the middle, small and poor peasants tend to work harder than the rich peasant class overall, women of the rich peasant class work longer than any other group. A reason for this is the need to prepare food for hired-in labour as well as enhanced livestock maintenance tasks, both within the household compound, in a context where it is not possible to hire-in female labour to assist with these tasks. The need to entertain guests more frequently to demonstrate their economic position further adds to women's domestic workloads. Papanek (1989) has termed this "status-production" work, where women work harder to improve household status as this has long-term pay-offs in terms of family welfare, thus contributing to their own future security.

Another interesting example of class/caste and gender intersections, with particular reference to the land question, comes from Gupta's (1997) research on land transactions and dowry payments in a West Bengal village. Given the tight monitoring of land sales, mortgages and transfers by the state, especially of redistributed land post-1977, dowry has become one way of informally accessing land. Dowry demands may be either in land or cash, though there is more pressure on landed households for payments of dowry in land. In a later study, Gupta (2002) found that 33 per cent of 870 households across four villages had lost land due to dowry demands, more valuable now due to technological innovations. This has led to devaluation if not outright ill-treatment of daughters in these families. In landless households dowry transactions are usually in cash, to invest in small businesses or improvements in labour here are clearly measurable, women tend to be valued more than in landed households.

Deshpande (2002:27), however, uses NSS data on per capita expenditures and NFHS-2 data on autonomy and decision-making to challenge the existence of a trade-off between autonomy and material prosperity in contemporary times. Comparing data across major social categories in India, she finds that while dalit women are materially worse off than upper caste women, they no longer seem to retain an edge in terms of autonomy and decision-making either (investment in health care and purchase of jewellery are the indicators used), though *adivasi* (indigenous) women seem to be slightly better off in this respect.

What seems clear is that assets under the control of men or women have different effects on the allocation of work and also expenditures within the household. Current patrilineal inheritance seems to favour boys over girls, but if daughters did have more resources at their disposal, it is likely that they would be valued more as potential sources of livelihood security.

Assessing Gains and Gaps in Project Experiences

In line with the multiple dimensions of poverty identified by the poor themselves, namely, lack of income and assets; sense of voiceless ness and powerlessness in the institutions of state and society, and vulnerability to adverse shocks [Chambers 1995], most international agencies have in the last five years modified their strategic objectives to reflect this broader understanding of poverty. IFAD, for instance, has now identified three strategic objectives: strengthening the capacity of the rural poor and their organisations; improving equitable access to productive resources and technology; and increasing access of the poor to financial assets and markets [IFAD 2002]. I focus on the first to two in the rest of this paper, as community organisations and user groups have now become a widely accepted strategy for implementation of projects concerned with asset creation and management.

Despite a formal commitment to gender

mainstreaming, that is, consideration of gender relations and gender differences in all stages of planning, implementation and monitoring of projects recent reviews and assessments across agencies reveal less than satisfactory performance in relation to these key objectives, from a gender perspective. Gender equality in most cases does not feature as an explicit goal of the project, and this may be because of the assumption that gender has been mainstreamed into the project design, yet in practice it leads to the exclusion of women, particularly form decision-making and control positions. In the IFAD-supported Orissa Tribal Development Project, for instance, self-Help groups (SHGs) were organised for women, while the Water User Society and Village Committee, from which they were excluded, were taking the major decisions. Women therefore soon lost interest in the SHDs, and the numbers did not increase beyond three. I analyse below a few project experiences with a view to drawing lessons for the future.

Bangladesh: Fisheries and Homestead Cultivation

Bangladesh has a high level of rural poverty, but also a network of NGOs implementing varied sets of interventions for poverty alleviation. It therefore offers some valuable insights in terms of enhancing development effectiveness. The findings from a study of the impacts of vegetable production and fishpond management technologies on household resource allocation, but also on women's empowerment, raise some interesting issues [Hallman et al 2003]. First, a certain level of material and non-material assets is a precondition for the adoption of new technologies, hence while a majority of the adopters were "poor" (55 per cent owned between 1-4.5 acres of land), the very poor (landless) were largely excluded. Secondly, while poor women were targeted for both the vegetable and fishpond intervention, the former, based on individual households was found to be more successful than the latter, based on group action. This was because of the lack of coordination and trust amongst group members, and misappropriation by the group leaders, who had been trained by the NGO, whereas other members had not. Further, while the vegetables were generally grown on the homestead plots and labour inputs could be flexibly timed, the ponds were at a distance from the homes and hence the women were not always able to go there regularly. A common constraint, however, was the public/private space dichotomy, with women not always able to retain control over the marketing of these products.

While fisheries, both inland (e.g., Bangladesh) and coastal (e.g., Sri Lanka and India), are seen to contribute to improving nutrition levels of the poor and providing a source of livelihood, there has been much recent debate about the commercialization and export-orientation of the fisheries sector and the coming in of large trawlers, which in fact deprive the poor of their livelihood. Inland prawn cultivation has caused land salinity and a destruction of other environmental resources, and has been challenged legally in both eastern India and parts of south-western Bangladesh. 7 While aquaculture is a readily accessible activity for women, they generally participate in low-skilled and low-paid jobs, have marginal access to training and extension services and are excluded from decision-making and control over resources. Gains, if at all, have been adhoc and unintended, rather than planned. As Agarwal (2001:1624) notes, participation can mean many different things from nominal involvement, activity-specific participation to playing much more active roles in decision-making. A gender-responsive policy would focus on ensuring shifts in their socio-economic status as well, and not just involving women and enhancing their workloads [AIT 2000].

India: Land and Poverty Reduction

In line with the new understanding of poverty and the focus 'on local institutions, 40 per cent of World Bank aided projects in India now depend on local organizations and user groups for their implementation. A study of three such projects (Sodic Lands Reclamation Project, UP; Forestry Project, MP; and the irrigation component of the Economic Restructuring programme, AP) in 2000 sought to understand the levels of inclusiveness and effectiveness of groups in these projects in terms of achievement and functioning indicators. While it is often assumed that user groups would foster inclusion of the disadvantaged in decision-making, equitable distribution of the resource in question and democratic governance and accountability, (apart from being cost-effective delivery mechanisms), this is not necessarily the case [Also et al 2002]. Participation appears to be highest amongst those already well connected and generally low amongst women, though this does not necessarily mean that they do not receive immediate benefits. While two-thirds of those interviewed gave a good rating to the achievement of formal objectives, whether distribution of inputs, forest protection or maintenance of the irrigation system, asset creation and equitable distribution got lower ranks. Transparency was limited and members were not aware of how funds were managed or decisions made, and in the event of any conflict, external backstops were needed to resolve it (ibid).

What these experiences reveal is that poverty targeting and equitable distribution of short-term benefits can be achieved even without higher levels of inclusion. Another good example of this comes from the Girijan Cooperative Corporation (GCC), formed as part of the Andhra Pradesh Tribal Development Programme (APTDP), financed by IFAD between 1991 and 2001, which focuses on the marketing of non-timber forest produce (NTFP), particularly gum, a major income generation activity for indigenous women. While the GCC has contributed considerably to women's employment and income, it does not have a specific gender dimension built into its programmes.

Nepal: Forest and Livestock

In its analysis of the specific outcomes of group-based development in terms of social inclusion and the empowerment of women, the Nepal Human Development Report [UNDP 2004:73] found that while most projects rate well in terms of enhancing livelihood conditions, their impact on social status is low. The main problems have been the exclusion of the ultra-poor, limitation of capacity-building to the group leaders (often the educated elite), lack of resources for scaling up, or indeed to ensure sustainability following project withdrawal. Further, most of these groups are concentrated in the hills (highest HDI), rather than the mountains or terai, and hence do not deal with geographical exclusion. These are also mostly low absentee areas, as it is likely that in high absentee ones, women's workloads would be higher and they would be unable to spare time for group activities and meetings.

One of the well documented group types are the community forestry user groups (CFUGs), registered with the department of forests. In Sindhupalchowk district, for instance, 76 per cent membership of the groups was male (only 663 out of 13,125 groups are female groups). In the executive committee, female membership was lower at 20 per cent. While these groups may have led to the fulfilment of environmental goals, they have not necessarily led to an improvement in gender relations. Inferiority based on illiteracy, gender or caste status, vulnerability and the lack of transparency in functioning facilitates elite dominance in these groups [Biggs et al 2004]. The growing realization of this male bias, has now led to moves to change membership guidelines to include all adults and reserve 33 per cent of executive positions for women.

Given the general scarcity of land, livestock has emerged as a major asset, particularly for women. Livestock development programmes, which did not simultaneously focus on fodder development, such as the Nepal Small Farmer Development Project, however, failed to meet their goals. In the later Nepal Hill Leasehold Forestry and Forage Development Project (HLFFDP, 1993-2003), livestock and fodder development were jointly undertaken, while also specifically targeting the landless, women-headed households and disadvantaged indigenous groups. Unlike the community forestry programmes involved a redistribution of assets to the poor by leasing degraded sites to specifically targeted groups of resource-poor households, identified jointly by NGO partners and supportive government officials. The objective was to enable forest rehabilitation while also increasing the supply of fodder and forage for livestock that would provide incomes to these households.

The evaluation of HLFFDP [IFAD 2003] found the poverty impact to be uneven, varying with location, dynamism of groups and potential of the plots, yet there was a significant increase in the ownership of goats, rather than mulch animals, due to improved access to forage. While two-thirds of the targeted households earned some income from goats, the impact of other income generating activities was insignificant. Women's collection time for fuel and fodder was also reduced substantially. While usufruct leases on these forest lands have been granted to them for 40 years, it is important now to clarify the conditional ties and secure the tenures.

Despite the fact that both forest and small livestock activities are essentially in women's domain, it is interesting to note that only 27 per cent of group members were women and 11 percent of leasehold groups were all-women groups, with others participating as wives of members [Lama 2005]. Yet the appointment of 46 women group promoters and gender training for forest rangers is gradually leading to enhanced gender sensitivity [IFAD 2003] and even where women are not decision-makers, they do attempt to influence decisions. The leasehold forestry project has been expensive to implement, and one of the key lessons emerging is to allow a bottom-up and participatory process of self-identification of the poorest, while also targeting a critical mass of households within a given area/cluster as remote locations particularly need sustained support. Benefits will not trickle down, hence proactive policies are needed to address the needs of the disadvantaged groups, and women within then. Skills in livestock management, production of forage seed and livestock improvement need to be provided specifically to women, along with marker linkages, if equity goals are to be met, alongside poverty goals. Experiences from Pakistan, Bangladesh and India, in similarly patriarchal settings, reveal that pursuing gender equality goals at all levels require policy commitment and programmatic leadership as "there is little built in incentive to pursue gender objectives—in fact the reverse, since concern with gender equity significantly slows implementation progress" [Mosse 1999:39].

Gender Mainstreaming: Institutional Lessons and Policy Directions

An assessment of the gender dimensions of World Bank assistance is 12 countries revealed that while the bank appears to have done the right things in Bangladesh over the last decade, consistent with national policies, the gender relevance of its policies in Sri Lanka were at best modest [OED 2002:3]. This is perhaps because the starting points have been education and health disparities, linked to maternity (important in Bangladesh though not so much in Sri Lanka), rather than labour market interventions or a holistic analysis and gender inequality. The evaluation of 53 project appraisal documents reveals that only a third had both a gender analysis of gender-disaggregated monitoring indicators, in the others, ad hoc WID components had been added on, predictably with mixed results. Process factors particularly have rarely been added on, predictably with mixed results. Process factors particularly have rarely been addressed in most monitoring systems.

I summarise below some policy options for enhancing both programme and institutional effectiveness.

(i) Women's legal entitlements to land need to be clarified to provide an enabling environment for gender equality. In India, the recommendations of the 17th Law Commission to remove the clauses that disadvantaged women in the Hindu Succession Act 1956 [Reddy et al 2000], have recently been approved by the Rajya Sabha (The Hindu, August 17, 2005), Yet specific references and incentives are needed to ensure the entitlements of both single and married women are actualized. It is also important to clarify rights to common property such as forests and village grazing lands, as these are key resources for certain groups such as tribes and nomadic pastoralists.

(ii) Mechanisms for implementation of laws and policies too need to be clarified. Societies are governed by plural systems of rules that influence behaviour and interactions at different levels. Land in particular, its links to kinship and lineage name, is subjected to community

norms, resulting in problems in the process of implementing legal rights awarded to women. It is important therefore to harmonies land, marriage and inheritance laws to ensure congruence and social acceptability on the one hand, while allowing plurality and openness in terms of mechanisms of enforcement. This would involve strengthening local conflict resolution mechanisms, while also making legal services easily accessible.

(iii) Access to "Khas" land and water resources, even though nominal in quantum, can play a symbolic if not substantive role in reiterating the value of women in the land sector. In India while policy commitment to this agenda has been affirmed since the Sixth Plan period (1980-85), lack of monitoring information limits any analysis of progress, which qualitative village studies show to be tardy.

(iv) Focus on human capital is a key to enable women to move away from low-income, low technology activities to more skilled and better paying tasks. Related to this, it is also important to identify assets and skills that are competitive in changing economic contexts and strengthen women's control therein.

(v) Organizing women appears as a key strategy for helping women gain access to assets- an essential means for building their confidence, leadership as well as bargaining power. This is because the process of claiming assets implies challenging the status quo with its consequent social risks, which becomes possible only when

women have substantial common interest and social support to take such action. Higher cluster level federation become important for ensuring not just forward and backward linkages, but also structural change.

(vi) Livestock and fodder development should be prioritized, as this again is a key asset for rural women being an insurance against risks and a from of savings and capital. Rather than attempting to ban goats as environmentally destructive, as was tried by the Andhra Pradesh government in India, it is much better to recognise their value for the poor, especially women, and try to overcome the negative environmental effects through provision of fodder and forage as done in Nepal.

(vii) Infrastructure development is as important as enhancing the productivity of natural resources (land, water, forests) or developing human and other assets, as it implies recognition of the premium on women's time and provides appropriate support to ease their burdens. Transport to the markets or from the fields and forests are major areas that affect women's well-being, as also the access to water and fuel. Performing these reproductive tasks in addition to a growing burden of productive work is likely to ultimately deplete women's body capital and negatively affect their capacity to work. Simultaneously, there is a need to encourage men to share in reproductive work, and essential part of livelihood strategies.

(viii) Focus on dealing with competitive markets is

essential to help women overcome the structural constraints to their equal economic participation. While women are often engaged in a range of productive tasks, restrictions on mobility prevent them from accessing the best markets directly, and they become dependent on their male relatives for this purpose.

(ix) Monitoring and evaluation should include quality and process factors and not just inputs and outputs. There is a need to specifically monitor how far gender has been mainstreamed in each programme component and the performance therein.

(x) One needs to get away from the notion that poverty reduction and gender equality can be achieved on the "cheap", with "micro investments" and small-scale interventions. The need for adequate investment of resources is a lesson that has emerged again and again from a range of sect oral interventions (literacy, for example), and is one that needs to be taken seriously. The Leasehold Forestry Project in Nepal, for instance, was seen to be expensive, yet its impact is likely to be more sustainable in the long run.

Conclusion

Progress towards gender equality through development intervention ultimately raises issues of the sustainability of gains. Most natural resource management projects are now based on the formation of user institutions. If these groups are to sustain and meet equity and collective action objectives then it is important to clarify their purpose, provide external support to build requisite capacities, form links with other local organizations and also address gender needs in the core activities of the project. While most projects set up infrastructure or invest in resource developing grassroot institutions with the capacity and resources to manage these newly created assets.

If empowerment of women is a goal, then this needs to be made explicit and the rules of engagement defined accordingly. People participate in accordance with their perception of benefits, hence if the focus in resource management programmes is primarily on physical works, as appears to be the case when one looks at monitoring formats, then it is no surprise that the better off would participate more actively than the landless or women, who have less to gain [Alsop 2004; Mosse 2005]. Further, development interventions often do not keep pace with the changing context of a globalised, competitive and market-driven world. In the case of women in particular, they continue to be pushed into traditional activities and micro-enterprises, with not much thought to market demand or sunrise activities. One needs to think afresh about rural women's work, about up scaling innovation, linking them with the knowledge economy and focusing equally on economic-structural concerns as on social-agency/capacity concerns.

Despite their lack of voice in many institutions, women belong to households, and as much research has demonstrated, while there are conflicts of interest between women and men, there are also substantial levels of cooperation and interest in mutual well-being.

So even where women have been excluded as members, their needs are often met. What appears clear however is that self-help and entrepreneurial strategies can only succeed in poverty reduction when the programme participant already has an initial asset base. Yet, access to assets alone is not enough, and for women particularly, long-term and differentiated support is essential to help them overcome constraints and engage in the public space of markets and state institutions.

While several projects have encouraged women to participate in development and decision-making processes by specifically targeting them, it is now recognized that a more gender–focused approach is necessary [Flintan 2003]. Women's groups do provide a forum for women to come together, share ideas, exchange information and develop a support network. Yet strategic shifts in access to resources and benefits (linked as they are to responsibilities for maintaining them), can only emerge if men too support such a shift, and take on a more equal share of both productive and reproductive work. In the context of structural reform, poor men too are facing a crisis in term of accessing productive assets, markets and income, leading to a crisis of masculinities that is often reflected in growing trends of violence against women. If gender equality is indeed to be achieved, there is need pay attention to the interests of women, but also to men and to shifts in gender relations occurring on account of contextual changes.

3

Microfinance is a 'Magic Bullet' for a Woman's Empowerment

Introduction

One of the workshops organised at the 2004 World Social Forum in Mumbai was provocatively entitled 'Is microfinance the magic bullet for women's empowerment? The answer to such a question is clearly no because there are no magic bullets in the policy world, development or otherwise. That such a question had to be posed is a testimony to the evangelism with which microfinance is promoted by many in the development community. At the same time, however, this evangelism appears to have triggered a dismissal of microfinance which is often as sweeping and as poorly grounded in evidence as the claims themselves [see discussion in Kabeer 2001]. Given this polarization, it is necessary to sift carefully through stories, assertions, opinions and anecdotes in support of one set of positions or the other in order to clarify what microfinance has achieved, and failed to achieve, in the lives of poor women.

There is a second set of debates in the field of microfinance that is of relevance to this paper. This is less about the merits or otherwise of microfinance and more about the philosophy that should underlie the provision of financial services as a way of illustrating the differences. She favours what she calls the "financial systems" approach which offers a commercially-oriented, minimalist package of financial services for the economically active poor -with sub sided job creation or charity for the rest. She is less well disposed towards what she presents as the alternative "poverty lending" approach which she identifies with donor-subsidized lending for the poor, particularly the poorest of the poor, often linked to training, social and other support services.

The imperatives of cost-recovery and financial sustainability which drive the financial systems approach clearly resonate with neo-liberal orientation to market principles. In is not surprising therefore that it has come to assume a hegemonic position in international development thinking about microfinance as a tool for poverty reduction. However, while it is clear that a financial systems approach makes fewer demands on donor funds or government subsidies than a poverty lending approach, it is by no means self-evident that it is also more effective in achieving poverty reduction or women's empowerment. The evidence on impacts reported by minimalist microfinance organisations as opposed to others which take a more "socially-oriented" approach is too mixed to allow for such an unambiguous conclusion.

The position taken in this paper is that the provision of financial services, like the provision of any development resource, represents a range of possibilities, rather than a predetermined set of outcomes. Which of these possibilities are realized in practice will be influenced by a host of factors, including the philosophy that governs their delivery, the extent to which they are tailored to the needs and interests of those they are intended to reach, the nature of the relationships which govern their delivery and that most elusive of all developmental inputs the calibre and commitment of the people who are responsible for delivery. The design of financial services to poor should be based on an empirically-based understanding of the relationship between context, approach and impact.

The aim of the paper is to contribute to such an understanding by examining the empirical evidence on the impact of microfinance with respect to poverty reduction and the empowerment of poor women. It is interested in the extent to which access to financial services helps poor women address their practical daily needs as well as their strategic gender interests and whether the approach taken makes a difference to these outcomes. However, the paper recognizes that strategic gender interests go to the very heart of the structures of patriarchal power: the abolition of a coercive gender division of labour; of unequal control over resources; ending male violence, women's control over their own bodies, the establishment of political equality and the ending of sexual exploitation [Molyneux 1985].

These are not structures that can be changed overnight. Instead, the process of transformation may need to begin more modestly with the constraints that prevent women from exercising their individual agency on a practical everyday basis. In any case, there may be many women for whom the desirability of this larger agenda of change, if they have thought about it at all, is likely to be overshadowed by the daily struggles for survival. Prioritizing strategic gender interests over their everyday practical needs may not only fail to reflect their own order of priorities, it may actively discourage their participation.

However, the two do not need be in opposition to each other. Meeting the daily practical needs for poor women in ways that transform the conditions in which they are empowered to take on some of the more deeply entrenched aspects of their subordination. In other words, how needs are addressed may be as critical as which needs are addressed in bringing about the larger structural transformation embodied in the idea of strategic gender interests [Kabeer 1999].

Poverty, Vulnerability and Social Exclusion

A static view of poverty defines it in terms of the capacity to meet basic needs. There is, however, increasing recognition of the need for a dynamic approach which allows for the possibility that meeting one's needs today does not guarantee that they will be met tomorrow. The concept of vulnerability draws attention to the basic uncertainty which surrounds the capacity of poor people to meet their needs on a regular and assured basis. Vulnerability may reflect exposure to short-term and idiosyncratic risks or it may be the product of long-standing, structural factors. The poor are more vulnerable than the rest of the population because they face a wider variety of risks and shocks and they have fewer resources to fall back on: Some poor households may seek to take precautionary measures, but have to live "diminished lives" as a result [Dreze and Sen 1991: 11]. Others seek to cope with crisis as and when it occurs.

Poverty and vulnerability are not purely economic phenomena, reflecting what people have they are also social phenomena, reflecting who they are. The south Asia region is characterized by various kinds of historically entrenched group-based inequalities. Caste, ethnicity and religion exacerbate the economic dimensions of poverty and vulnerability through process of cultural devaluation which assign certain groups of people a lower position in the social hierarchy.

Gender inequalities cut across different strata of society. Broadly speaking, dominant cultural norms and values in south Asia stress male responsibility for protecting and providing for household members and construct women as their life-long dependents. Men are given authority within the household and prior claim to its resources. For poorer men, however, the failure to fulfill their gender ascribed roles, to live up to social expectations about their capacity to protect and provide can lead to considerable stress and demoralization on their part as well as domestic violence, high levels of alcoholism, abandonment of their families and responsibilities.

Women, on the other hand, can expect to be provided for, but are assigned a subordinate status within their households and in society at large. Devalued by the prevailing culture, denied equal access to resources, facing cultural restrictions on their physical mobility, women's dependent status leaves them open to what Cain et al (1979) termed "patriarchal risk", the likelihood of abrupt declines in their economic welfare and social status should they find themselves bereft of male guardianship. The greater their dependence, the greater the risk.

However, women from disadvantaged social groups do my always face the same degree of cultural restrictions on their physical mobility as women from more affluent or higher caste households and are more likely to engage in paid work outside the home. They may not be economically dependent to the same degree, but as members of poor and socially marginalized groups, the face various kinds of gender discrimination from members of their own community as well as more powerful actors across in the institutional spectrum.

Microfinance Strategies for Poverty Reduction: Markets and Movements

It is this context of insecure livelihoods and limited options that gives rise to the need for financial services of a particular kind among the poor, services that will permit them to translate "small pay-ins" into "large take-outs" when needed [Rutherford 2002]. The "pay-ins" take the form of regular contributions to savings and loan repayments in the amounts that they can manage while the "take outs" are lump sums of money in the form loans or accumulated savings which can tide households over an emergency or a period of scarcity, or finance life cycle events (birth, marriages, burials) or used to purchase productive and other assets. However, these lump sums, though large from the perspective of the poor, are too minuscule, and the associated "pay-ins" even more so, to appeal to formal financial providers. The poor are in any case dismissed by them as unreliable and hence un bankable. Institutional exclusion from formal financial provision leaves poor households dependent on informal financial services, often at usurious rates of interest which can send them spiralling into a vicious cycle of impoverishment and debt.

Microfinance organizations (MFOs) serve to address this dual phenomenon of institutional exclusion, on the one hand, and adverse incorporation, on the other. However, as we have noted, they vary considerably in their philosophy, their vision and their strategies. At the "market" end of the spectrum are those who perceive the problem to be one of failure in financial markets as a result of asymmetrical information and who therefore seek to provide market-like alternatives to excluded groups. These are closer to the "financial systems" approach and exemplified in the south Asian context by Association for Social Advancement (ASA), Bangladesh and Society for Helping Awakening Rural Poor through Education (SHARE), India.

At the other "movements" end of the spectrum are organisation which perceive the problem of financial exclusion to be symptomatic of deep-rooted structural inequalities which not only curtail access to formal financial provision but also the capacity to participate in other aspects of social life. Their vision and organisational strategies seek to address these inequalities. They are closer to the "poverty lenders" approach and exemplified by Centre for Youth and Social Development (CYSD) in the south Asian context.

Other MFOs fall somewhere along this spectrum.]

Most MFOs in the south Asian context, regardless of where they are on this continuum, deal primarily with women and take a group-based approach to service provision. However, they vary in their approach to group formation. Some have adapted the Grameen Bank model of the group, e.g., SHARE, other promote self-help groups (Professional Assistance for Development Action, PRADAN and CYSD) and still others work with a co-operative structure (Self Employed Women's Association (SEWA) and Credit and Development Forum (CDF)). They also vary between those like SHARE which offer a minimalist credit-centered programmed and those which link financial services with other forms of provision. Some like PRADAN offer primarily livelihood-based services while others like Bangladesh Rural Advancement Committee (BRAC) may also offer social and legal services. And finally, MFOs vary in whether they are concerned primarily with economic goals or whether, like BRAC and CYSD, they have a broader social mission as well.

Given their financial focus, we would expect most MFOs to have some economic impact on the lives of the poor, However, there are reasons to expect certain social consequences as well. One is that the majority of MFOs work with women from poor households and often from socially excluded groups. Hence they have the potential to address social inequality. The second reason relates to their group-based strategies. These hold out the possibility for bringing about social change for the simple reason that people acting together are often able to achieve what they cannot achieve individually. This is as true of the privileged sections of a society as it is of the marginalised find it far harder to undertake forms of collective action which might help to address their social disadvantage.

MFO strategies offer them the possibility of belonging to a group of their choosing in contrast to the society ascribed or economically imposed relationships which tend to make up the bulk if their experience of marginalization and to gain access to knowledge about the world beyond the confines of their immediate experience. Such strategies could, in principle, serve to empower them, both individually and collectively. Whether they do so in practice is a matter for empirical investigation. This paper analyses various attempts at such investigation in order to come up with some answers. It draws on studies carried out under the Impact programme on BRAC from Bangladesh and SHARE (Andhra Pradesh), CYSD (Orissa) and PRADAN (Jharkhand) as well as on the wider literature from the region.

Outreach and Impact

Microfinance Outreach

The first question to ask in a review essay of this kind is who precisely gains access to microfinance services. The consensus appears to be that the majority of organisations do not reach, and sometimes actively exclude, the extreme poor [Hulme and Mosley 1996]. This is supported by recent studies carried out by the Consultative Group to Assist the Poorest (CGAP) in a number of countries which found that a sizeable percentage of households that had newly joined an

MFO (i.e., before they had benefited from access to financial services) were not drawn from the poorest 30 per cent of the population in the context in which the organization worked.

In the Indian context, the CGAP studies suggest that SHARE, with its minimalist Grameen model, did better than PRADEN, which combines self-help group formation with livelihood support, in drawing on the poorest third of the population in areas in which they worked [Sharma et al 2000, Somanathan 2003]. However, this conclusion would be misleading because the CGAP studies measure relative rather than absolute poverty. Given that incidence of poverty in Andhra Pradesh, where SHARE is based, was about 11 per cent according to official statistics and around 44 per cent in Bihar/Jharkhand where the PRADAN study was carried out, it is highly possible that group members recruited by SHARE from the poorest tercile were generally less poor than the majority of group members who joined PRADAN. This is supported by Imp-Act studies which showed that over 75 per cent of households in the areas in which PRADAN worked had experienced food shortages in the areas in which PRADAN worked had experience food shortages in the previous year compared to less than 10 per cent of households in SHARE's area of operation [Kabeer and Noponen 2004; Cortijo and Kabeer 2004].

SHARE's minimalist approach was clearly successful in drawing on the poorest households in the more dynamic state of Andhra Pradesh with its relatively low levels of poverty but may not have performed quite as well as PRADAN self-help group approach in the extremely poor and physically isolated areas of Jharkhand. Both organisations, however, reported high levels of social excluded groups among its membership: 97 per cent of PRADAN's membership and 83 per cent of SHARE's belonged to adivasis, dalits and "other backward castes".

A study of CYSD carried out in Koraput, one of the poorest districts in India's poorest state, found that it was the savings focus of self-help groups that attracted women form very poor households. However, it also found that what persuaded women to join a group was not necessarily what kept them together over time. Thus 93 per cent of new members cited a safe place to keep their savings as their reason for joining a self-help group compared to 23 per cent who mentioned access to emergency loans and less than 1 per cent who spoke of group unity. By contrast, only 63 per cent of longer standing members mentioned access to emergency loans and 17 per cent mentioned group unity.

There is also evidence from Bangladesh that supports the view that the extreme poor may require a different set of interventions than the moderately poor. BRAC found that its "mainstream" rural development programmes was largely by-passing the very poor. It therefore developed a programme combining monthly food transfers, savings, credit and training over a period of years targeted explicitly to this group. While it could be argued that the able-bodied extreme poor will gain more from wage employment and public works than from attempts to promote their entrepreneurship, this is less easily extended to poor women in regions where there are cultural restrictions on their public mobility.

Economic Impact of Microfinance

Reviews of microfinance efforts from various parts of the world suggests that, by and large, access to microfinance has had a positive economic impact, that this impact has been often larger for those closer to the poverty line than those further away and that they increase with duration of membership or intensity of loans as members begin to invest in assets rather than consumption [Morduch and Haley 2001, and Mosley 1996], However, there are also examples to suggest that programmes specially designed to serve the needs of the extreme poor can overcome some of the constraints associated with broader interventions.

Findings from the Imp-Act programme provide evidence on economic impact in the south Asian context. These studies confirm that access to financial services generally improved the economic position of households; improving asset base and diversification into higher return occupations among SHARE members in Andhra Pradesh [Todd 2001]; Promoting the adoption of new agricultural practices and significant increases in income among CYSD SHGs in Orissa [Dash and Kabeer 2004]; promoting irrigation and other new agricultural practices, in creasing ownership of livestock and levels of savings and reducing reliance on moneylenders among PRADAN SHG members in Jharkhand [Kabeer and Noponen 2004]. Murthy et al's study (nd) of SAPAP self-help groups in Andhra Pradesh also reported an overall reduction in poverty, including reductions among the extreme poor.

While women's needs and interests cannot be equated with impact at the household level, they are not independent of them either, women, along with other members of their households, have a stake in the overall prosperity and well-being achievements of their households. However, we are also interested in how these gains are achieved and distributed. There is a string possibility that in contexts where there are strong restrictions on women's public mobility, many of the documented economic consequences reflect male rather than women's agency and may have little impact on intra-household inequalities.

Goetz and Sen Gupta (1996) found that 63 per cent of women loan holders surveyed in their Bangladesh study of three microfinance programmes had exercised "partial" very limited or no control" in relation to loan use and conclude that they exercised very little voice in household decision-making. However, they do not indicate whether women's say in household decision-making had increased or declined with access to loans and moreover, as Zaman (1996) points out, their findings could equally plausibly be interpreted as showing that 61 per cent of the respondents had "full, significant or partial control" and hence a fair degree of control.

Kabeer (2001) found that the economic agency exercised by women loan holders with the SEDP in Bangladesh varied with household wealth, with women from better-off household exercising a greater decision-making role in loan-supported activities that poorer women. However, wives of male loan holders were found to exercise the lowest levels of economic contribution varied by organisation, with Grameen loan holders reporting higher levels of contribution than BRAC. Once again non-loan holders reported the least levels of contribution.

In India, the study of SHARE by Todd reported that the vast majority of its clients engaged in economic activity, regardless of duration of membership, an indication of the poverty of their households. However, duration of membership reduced women's reliance on casual wage labour and increased their engagement in more profitable forms of self-employment , including animal husbandry. As Todd notes, investment in livestock was one of the pathways to higher income among SHARE clients.

The CYSD study also found high levels of economic activity among both old and new members but a greater diversification our of subsistence agriculture among older members as well as lower rates of seasonal migration. The analysis of PRADAN suggested that membership of PRADAN had reduced women's reliance on unskilled wage labour activity and increased their involvement in their own cultivation.

Murthy et al's study (nd) of SAPAP self-help groups in Andhra Pradesh noted evidence of increased employment opportunities over time among group members, an improvement in the quality of work available as well as diversification into new, non-traditional activities.

MFOs can play an important role as conduit for new forms of knowledge and information, an important causal factor in promoting women's economic agency. This is likely to be particularly important in remote rural areas such as those where both CYSD and PRADAN worked. In the area covered by the CYSD study, for instance, over 60 per cent of the sample of both mature and new members had never listened to a radio while only 1 per cent read newspapers. Not surprisingly, CYSD was a major source of new information. Dash and Kabeer found that mature CYSD members were more likely to know how to undertake bank transactions and to deal with government agencies those new members. They also found that mature members were more likely to have adopted land building, bio manure, HYV seeds, compost pit, commercial vegetable cultivation and multiple cropping than new members , suggesting that some of the practical information provided by CYSD had been translated into practice. PRADAN played a similar role on Jharkhand. Kabeer and Noponen (2004) found that PRADAN members were far more likely than non-members to be able to count large currency notes, to sign their names and to calculate interest rates. They also reported a higher rate of adoption of improved livelihood practices.

Social Impact of Microfinance

The review of impact studies by Morduch and Haley (2001) provides examples of the social impact MFOs, have had including a number located in the south Asian context. These include health, nutrition and education. The Imp-Act studies also provide evidence of MFOs' social impact. Studies of PRADAN and CYSD, both located in remote and highly food insecure regions, report significant improvements in food security and quality of diet, access to clean drinking water and improvements in housing. The study of SHARE also noted nutritional improvements and improved housing. Murthy et al (nd) found that members of SAPAP self-help groups in Andhra Pradesh reported improvements in regularity of meals, levels of child nutrition and lower levels of infant mortality in the past five years.

Where findings are disaggregated by gender, it is possible to ascertain to what extent the social impact also encompassed gender disparities. Thus Murthy et al (nd) noted that women members were more likely to report eating together with male members of the family, less likely to report disparities in food distribution and less likely to report severe malnutrition among girl children or female infant deaths in the past year. Loans to women, however, had positive and significant effects on children's status with a strong effect for girls than boys. Loans to men did not have such an impact. BRAC studies reported decline in severe malnutrition among children with stronger effects for girls than boys.

While children's education is frequently found to improve with access to microfinance, the findings on gender disparities are not consistent. Some reinforce the importance of loans to women for both general but also gender-equalizing result. Khandker (1999), for instance, found that a 1 per cent increase in loans to women borrowers with the Grameen Bank increased the probability of school enrolment by 1.9 per cent for girls and 2.4 per cent for boys while a 1 per cent increase in credit to male loan holders increased boy's enrolment by 3.1 per cent but had no effect on girls.

Kabeer (1999) found that children of women loan holders with the SEDP were more likely to be at school that children of male loan holders. In addition, women loan holders with the SEDP were more likely to be at school that were male loan holders. The presence of BRAC within a village was found to increase overall enrolment rates by 6 per cent, and girls' schooling programmes rather than access to credit per se.

In India, two separate studies of SHARE [Todd 2001, Cortijo and Kabeer 2004] both found that while SHARE membership had a positive effect on boys' education, it had almost no effect on girls. In fact, Cortijo and Kabeer found that mature SHARE members were more likely than new members to report involvement in waged labour and other forms of paid work as a primary or secondary occupation. Andhra Pradesh has of course the highest levels of child labour in India so the findings suggest that while SHARE was contributing to its reduction, its effect was confined to boys' labour.

Nor was it necessarily the case that more socially-oriented MFOs reported greater gender equality in their impact. In the case of CYSD SHGs, children of new members reported higher levels of literacy and greater likelihood of going to school than mature members. On the other hand, Kabeer and Noponen (2004) found that children of PRADAN group members more likely to go to school than children of non-members. Moreover, while a higher percentage of boys went to school than girls for both member and non-members, the gender gap was smaller for PRADAN members.

Gender and Power within Households

Claims that participation in microfinance activities has implications for women's empowerment within the household were investigated by a number of studies with varying results. Intra-household decision-making was one commonly investigated indicator of women's empowerment. While there is evidence that microfinance can have an impact on women's role in household decision-making, it has not occurred evenly in all contexts or in all areas of decision-making.

Kabeer (2001) found that male loan holders with SEDP generally reported sole decision-making in relation to use of loans, the running of loan-funded enterprise and disposal of income from these enterprises, suggesting that wives of male loan holders did not have a great deal of say on these matters. While SEDP's women loan holders did appear to exercise a greater degree of say than the wives of male loan holders, they were more likely to report joint and less likely to report sole decision-making than male loan holders.

According to Hashemi et al, both membership of Grameen Bank or BRAC and duration of membership had significant positive effects on involvement in major decisions within the family as well in making large and small purchases.

In India, the study of CYSD found that membership of SHGs had little impact on patterns of household decision-making. In the case of PRADAN as well, there was little difference found in own or joint decision-making between members and non-members but where differences were found to be statistically significant, they did not provide evidence of positive impact. PRADAN members were found to be less likely to participate in decisions about family size and visiting their natal family than non-PRADAN members. However, a further comparison between those SHG members who had or had not participate in PRADAN's livelihood support programme found that the additional support significantly strengthened women's sole decision-making role on a wider range of different decisions, including children's education, choice of livelihood activity, use of loans, purchase and sale of assets and visits to natal family.

Murthy et al (nd) reported that SAPAP self-help group members were far more likely than non-members to report making decision about a range of "reproductive rights" issues, particularly the decision to have an abortion, but also the nature of the contraception, how many children to have and the age of marriage for their daughter.

Holvoet (2005) carried out one of the more carefully designed studies of the impact on decision-making in the context on Tamil Nadu. She compared patterns of decision–making for three groups of women: MYRADA-organised SHG members who received loans from the WDP since 1993-94 and represented a more recent cohort of loan holders; SHG members organised by MYRADA and RIDO who had received loans from the Tamil Nadu government's Women's Development Programme since 1990-91 and represented an older cohort; and a third group made up of women and men who received individual loans from the government's IRDP programme. She explored a number of different areas of decision-making male dominated decision-making, norm-following decision-making and bargaining over decisions.

She found that channeling loans through women's groups rather than to individual women substantially increased the likelihood of female decision-making and bargaining relative to the case for loan use, money management, time and task allocation and decisions related to cottage industry. While the timing of loans to women who belonged to MYRADA groups made little difference to patterns of decision-making, a comparison of RIDO and MYRADA groups who has both accessed loans at the same time suggested that, along with membership of groups, the strategy for group organisation had an important effect on findings. The shift from norm following to bargaining for different areas of decision-making was far more striking for MYRADA than for RIDO group members. Thus, the study supports the view that not only does group-based lending to women have a greater effect on intra-household decision-making than individual lending but also that strategy used in group formation (such as frequency of meetings, investment in group formation, more intensive training) is also likely to make more of a difference than duration of group membership per se.

The issue of domestic violence is another area that has featured in investigations of the impact on intra-household that microfinance has had. Once again, finings vary. Goetz and Sen Gupta suggest an increase in domestic violence but offer only anecdotal evidence. However, an ethnographic study by Rahman did provide quantitative an qualitative evidence to this effect (1999). He reported that out of 120 women borrowers with Grameen Bank in one village, 18 per cent reported a decrease in violence while 70 per cent reported an increase in violence within the household as a result of their involvement with the bank.

On the other hand, Hashemi et al found that women loan holders in their sample reported lower levels of domestic violence than did women in a control group—9-13 per cent compared to 21-27 per cent. They found that one route by which this apparent decline appears to have occurred was the increased awareness on the part of family members that women now had a public forum in which to discuss matters which had previously been private. A BRAC study reported higher levels of domestic violence among members than the comparison group (9 per cent compared to 6 per cent), but found that violence declined with duration of membership and with the additional of training to credit provision to levels lower than that of the comparison group (3.4 per cent).

Kabeer's analysis of response by women loan holders of the SEDP reported that most women felt that violence had gone down as a result of women's access to loans for a number of reason: the easing of economic stress had reduced one of the causes of violence and the fact that women were now seen to be sharing the responsibility for family provisioning with men rather than constituting part of male responsibility. Women also felt that they had greater bargaining power within the family and could (and did) withhold co-operation if husbands proved extremely abusive.

In the Indian context, the PRADAN study did not find any significant difference in the incidence of domestic violence reported by members and non-members. However, Murthy et al (nd) assessment of SAPAP found that 64 per cent of non-members reported domestic violence, with 29 per cent reporting wife beating, compared to just 45 per cent of SAPAP members who reported domestic violence, with 14 per cent mentioning wife beating.

Other studies provide other kinds of insights into

the impacts in terms of intra-household relations. The CYSD study found that not only were mature members more likely to believe that their economic contributions within the family were highly significant than new members but they were also more likely to report that their family members shared this view. PRADAN members were less likely to non-members to report pressure to bear sons ad more likely to keep back part of their income to dispose of. Murthy et al found that a higher percentage of members reported the freedom to visit and invite their parents and siblings and while a much lower percentage of both members and non-members said that they allowed adolescent daughters as much freedom as they allowed sons, members were still more likely to report such freedom.

Wider Social Impact

A less researched impact relates to the likelihood of changes beyond the individual member and her family to relationship in the wider community and policy domain. These were touched on in a number studies carried out under the Imp-Act programme. However, in contexts where different types of developmental organisations were active, it became necessary to separate out the consequences associated with different interventions. The study of BRAC by Kabeer and Matin (2004) found that many BRAC members were also members of at least one other NGO. Using regression analysis to control for alternative NGO membership, they found high levels of trust in other group members, regardless of number of years of BRAC membership, but that older group members were significantly more likely to express trust in relation to members of the ward-level federation of BRAC groups as well as members of other religions.

The study also found that years of BRAC membership increased levels of trust expressed in locally elected male as well as women members of the union parishad and its chairman and reduced the likelihood of having paid a bribe. It also increased likelihood of access to government programmes, of voting in national and local elections and of accurately naming the local level elected women representative.

It was clear from the study that type of group membership mattered. Controlling for membership of other NGOs allowed the separation of benefits/ consequences from different forms of membership and suggested that these could be mainly attributed to years of membership of BRAC. Since these other NGOs tended to be far more minimalist MFOs than BRAC (most frequently ASA and Grameen) this is not surprising.

Cortijo and Kabeer (2004) also used regression analysis to control for the fact that many of SHARE's members (40 per cent of mature and 31 per cent of new SHARE members) were also members of the government's DWCRA programme in the areas of Andhra Pradesh where their study was conducted. Their results suggested that membership of SHARE groups led to an improvement in business relationships within the community while DWCRA memberships was more strongly associated with general relationships with the rest of the community. Membership of DWCRA was also associated with increased likelihood of women having access to government programmes for the poor, of meeting with various elected and government officials, of attending various public meetings (gram sabha, janma bhumi and collectors grievance day), of participating in political protests and campaigns and of the ability to name the mandal president and the prime minister of the country. SHARE membership had a weaker or negligible effect on the likelihood of members voting at the local gram panchayat elections.

Qualitative findings from Todd's study appear to corroborate these results. Based on her interviews with a number of SHARE membership had increased their self-confidence and entrepreneurial activities and brought them greater respect within the community, the majority had no active involvement in community affairs and no desire to get involved.

Both CYSD and PRADAN work with some of the poorest and most socially excluded sections of India's population and represented the only forms of developmental group activity in the areas studies. Levels of participation in the formal public domain were found to be extremely low in these areas, regardless of whether or not they were members of SHGs, a reflection of their overall isolation. The traditional panchayat system did not function particularly effectively in these villages and village-level gram sabha meetings were held on a very irregular basis.

However, given these low overall levels of participation, PRADAN membership made a difference. Eleven per cent of PRADAN members had attended such a meeting compared to just 1 per cent of non-members and 15 per cent had approached a bank for an individual loan (indicative of the exercise of individual initiative) compared to just 2 per cent of non-members. These differences were both statistically significant. The CYSD study also found higher percentages of mature CYSD members relative to newer ones had interacted with government officials in order to address some problem and had participated in the palli sabha and gram sabha meetings, although as in the PRADAN context, overall levels of participation were low.

Dash and Kabeer also explored various forms of political agency on the part of CYSD members. It found that the percentages voting in elections were highest at local level ward level, for the sarpanch, for the samity member and zilla election, with mature members reporting significantly higher levels of participation than new members: generally between 80 and 90 percent. Percentages voting declined at higher levels (legislative assembly and national elections) and differences between mature and new member disappeared. Much lower percentages of both mature members generally reported significantly higher percentages of participation in election campaigns as well as the desire to context a local election. The differences were statistically significant.

Finally, the study found that while overall levels of participation in protests and campaigns were low, 43 per cent of mature members and 37 per cent of new members had taken part in protests against the making and selling of liquor while 55 per cent of mature and 30 per cent of new members had participated in anti-liquor campaigns within their community. Interest in this issue has to be interpreted in terms of the strong relationship between male alcoholism and violence against women as well as the drain that alcohol consumption represented on family resources. Education was the other issue around which members were active, with mature members reporting higher levels of activity than new. Such action generally took the form of demands for schools under as well as protests against teacher irresponsibility.

Murthy et al (nd) explored the "sociability" impact of participation in MFO groups in Tamil Nadu. They reported that 91 per cent of members had visited new places in the previous five years compared to 31 per cent of non-members; 83 per cent reported an increase in friendships compared to 26 per cent of non-members, with a higher percentage of the former reporting friends from other castes. While 34 per cent of dalit members reported caste-based violence in the public domain compared to 23 per cent of dalit non-members, 64 per cent of dalit members reported that group membership had reduced caste-based violence compared to 25 per cent of dalit non-members.

The study also reported that 95 per cent of the group members had voted during the last panchayat elections, many discussing the pros and cons of candidates during group meetings and around 15 per cent said that they had abided by decision taken during these forums. Women members had contested between 20 and 25 per cent of reserved seats for women during the 2001 elections. Only 18 per cent had won but the process of contesting elections had been an important experience, both for those who ran and for those who voted for them.

Poverty Reduction and Social Change

The far-ranging impact of microfinance has been discussed in this paper, some positive, some negative and some more consistent than others, Evidence that financial services help to protect livelihoods by regularizing income flows and reducing variability in consumption levels appears to be fairly consistent across a range of different approaches to financial service provision.

There are also consistent findings that microfinance helps to meet a variety of basic needs and promotes improvements in standards of living. We noted such evidence in relation to household food security and diversity of diet, to quality of housing and access to clean water. While there is generally positive evidence in terms of children's health, nutrition and education, the findings on gender disparities in these outcomes are weaker and less consistent.

The findings in this paper partly support Hulme and Mosley's contention that poverty impact tends to be strongest for those closest to the poverty line and weaker for those further away (1996). Security of consumption needs, and the capacity to cope with crisis, may have to be built up before poor households are prepared to take risks. However, findings from both Imp-Act and other studies challenge the apparent corollary implication drawn by Hulme and Mosley as well as Robinson (2001) that the extreme poor will not benefit from access to financial services. They suggest instead that the extreme poor can also benefit from financial services provided these are designed with their needs and constraints in mind.

As far as women's economic agency is concerned,

the evidence reported in this paper is positive, but there are exceptions as well as variations in the nature and strength of impact by context and by organisation. Financial services were found to promote women's participation in paid work in contexts where they may have been economically active but faced limited options. The evidence also suggests an increased voice in household decision-making, in some cases, as sole decision-maker and in others, in joint decision-making. In other cases, however, decision-making impact was negligible. Access to financial services was found to exacerbate domestic violence in some cases but to lead to a decline in others as a result of an increase in the size of women's economic contribution, or in the duration of membership or with the introduction of training and other services.

A number of studies also reported gender-related impacts in the wider community. These included improvements in relationships within the community, access to government services as well as political participation, protests and campaigns. They also included higher levels of trust towards fellow group members, towards elected officials as well as towards members of other castes and religious groups.

One of the limitations of conventional impact studies is that they tend to compare current participants of microfinance programme either by loan cycle or duration of membership or else in relation to non-participants. While such studies have often documented various sources of dissatisfaction with the programmes as well as negative or negligible outcomes along with evidence of their positive impact, they do embody a "selection bias" towards the views of those who stay within programmes against those who have left.

Attention to the views of those who have left the programme can help to correct this bias, but this is less frequently done. A review of "exit" studies carried out in relation to some of the organisations associated with the Imp-Act programme found both individual and programme-related reasons featured in explanations given for exit. In the case of SHARE, the only south Asian organisation included in the review, the reasons given included the amount of time spent at weekly meetings, the requirement of having to guarantee each other' loans, expulsion for falling behind on repayments, failure of their businesses, particularly among those who had no prior experience, and in a few cases, displeasure that people from all castes were permitted to join SHARE's groups [Todd 2001].

However, it should be added that a study of ex-clients, made up as it is of those who have chosen to leave or been expelled from an organisation, might be expected to be biased towards those with very negative views of the organisation. But Todd found than 30 per cent of the ex-clients were willing to return to SHARE without any conditions, while another 40 per cent were willing to return if some changes were made in organisational practices.

Finally, it should be pointed out what while there is reasonably robust evidence that access to microfinance leads to both direct economic and social improvements within the household, as well as changes in relationships in the wider community, there is less evidence to support the view that it helps poor people to "grow" out of poverty and graduation towards mainstream financial services is less robust. This may partly reflect lack of attention to such longer-term consequences in existing literature, but it should also raise questions about the limits to microfinance as well as the persistence of exclusionary barriers within formal.

Pathways to Change: Resources and Relationships

Analysis of the pathways through which the various direct and wider social benefits/consequences occur can make an important contribution to our understanding of processes of social change. It also contributes to policy debates about the philosophy and practice of microfinance for the poor. One obvious and direct route through which change occurred in the studies reviewed was via increased access to economic resources, both the financial services provided as well as the expanded levels of economic activity that these made possible.

A second direct route related to the provision of others services often linked to financial service often linked to financial service delivery, such as livelihoods support, health and legal training. They served to bring about cognitive and behavioural changes which interacted with, and amplified, changes brought about by access to financial services. The fact that these resources and services were channelled through women in contexts in which women have often been denied independent access to economic resources and had limited access to services meant that these routes also brought about important gender-related changes.

Along with these more easily attributable changes

associated with MFO activities, however, there were other changes which could not be tracked as easily to the provision of financial services because they operated through less easily discernible "relational" pathways. The provision of financial and other resources does not occur in a social vacuum, it occurs in the context of specific social relationships and promotes changes in others. These relationships, the experiences and the interactions associated with them, can in turn bring about changes which are only partly related to the financial services in question.

Two specific sets of social relations are directly associated with the provision of financial services. The first relate to interactions with the staff of the organizations in question, interactions which carry the potential for bringing about both the intended changes of the organisation through training, motivational and other activities. They also carry the potential for unanticipated changes through, for instance, offering new role-models for women to aspire to or providing a forum for interactions between poorer and less poor sections of the community which need not (necessarily) be based on client principles of deference and authority.

The second set of social relations are those between members of the groups organised by MFOs. However, these groups do not embody the same principles of organisation or the same kind of relationships between members. For instance, Thornton et al (2000) noted this in their review of some of the larger NGOs in Bangladesh. They distinguished between: *(i)* those organisation which were largely focused on the provision of financial services (such as Grameen Bank and ASA), *(ii)* those like BRAC which combined financial provision with a range of social, legal and other services; and *(iii)* those like Nijera Kori which had group savings but otherwise eschewed financial services and focused on social mobilisation.

They noted that the group meetings organised by the minimalist financial organisations' programmes were largely taken up with matters relating to loan disbursement and repayment. Since members were required to act as guarantors of members' loans meetings were often charactersied by some amount of tension and conflict. By contrast, group meetings orgainsed by Nijera Kori generally focused on training and reflection on economic and social issues of concerns to members. They tended to be more relaxed that to cover a wide range of topics.

Some of the Imp-Act studies also highlight differences in the group culture of different organisations. The BRAC study carried out by Kabeer and Matin reported that mature members observed with regret that the nature of group meetings had changed after BRAC began to expand its lending operations in the mid-1990s and to concern itself with financial sustainability and repayment rates. Earlier meetings now had a much narrower focus on loan disbursements and repayments.

SHARE's weekly meetings generally focus on loan-related matter. Interviews with 109 ex-clients found that 40 per cent gave the length of the meetings as their reason for leaving meetings were often not brought to a close until all members had paid their loan instalments. Another 22 per cent objected to group pressure to repay loans while some others left because husbands objected to the requirement that groups must jointly cover any arrears by individual members.

Loan-related concerns play a much smaller role in the formation of self-help groups of the kind organised, for instance, by PRADAN and CYSD. The CYSD study provides useful insights into the process of group formation as one means by which social change can be brought about [Dash and Kabeer 2004].

It suggested that CYSD did not necessarily build new social relations from scratch since strong ties already existed between members of isolated tribal communities, but it did help to diversify associational life within the community and to promote new ways of taking collective decisions, new resources share and new forms of leadership.

We would expect to find that the nature of organisational relationships promoted by MFOs will have implications for the kinds of impact they are able to achieve, particularly the social impact. This is partly supported by some of the evidence cited in this paper. We reported, for instance, Holvoet's finding that membership of particular kinds of self-help groups (MYRADA) had a for greater impact on women's role in intra-household decision-making than membership in other kinds of self-help groups (RIDO).

We also found that it was membership of BRAC, with its combination of Grameen style groups and linked social and legal services, rather than the other more minimalist MFO groups to which some BRAC members simultaneously belonged, that explained a series of wider benefits, including the likelihood of voting in local and national elections, reduced likelihood of having paid a bribe in the previous year, improved access to government programmes for the poor and higher levels of trust in elected officials.

On the other hand, we found that changes directly attributable to membership of SHARE were largely confined to women's greater sense of self-confidence within the household and improved business relations within the community. Others forms of wider impacts, including improvements in relations with the wider community, participation in local village assemblies, interaction with local government officials and participation in campaigns were generally more strongly associated with membe:ship of DWCRA, with SHARE membership reinforcing the change in some, but not all, cases.

VIII

Alternative Approaches to Microfinance

The analysis in this section suggests that financial services can play an important role in the lives of poor women but that their philosophy and design will determine the extent to which they promote women's well-being and agency as well as their longer-term capacity to reflect and act on their strategic interests.

However, the implications of this are difficult to raise and to explore in the face of the growing hegemony of the "financial system approach" among donors and governments.

There are understandable reasons for the appeal of the latter approach. In comparison with the patronage, corruption, leakages and default rates which characterised earlier subsided credit delivery to the poor by governments as well as the welfarist philosophy which underpinned so many programmes for women, an approach which stresses commercial principle as the basis for lending and financial sustainability as the organisational goal offers some obvious advantages.

Moreover, such organisations may well be better suited to certain contexts than the poverty lending approach. In contexts characterised by a vibrant local economy, functioning markets in goods and services and the absence of entrenched inequalities in the economic opportunities and life chances of specific social groups, a financial systems approach may not only succeed in compensation for any short-term failures in financial markets, but may serve in the long run to create a more integrated financial system. In such contexts, women with entrepreneurial capacity may have as much to gain from a financial systems approach as men.

However, the financial systems approach, with its roots in methodological individualism and a "competitive equilibrium" view of the world, is best able to deal with the financial exclusion of the poor when it reflects individual deficits (of assets, education, health, etc.) and market failure (problem of asymmetric information and contract enforcement). It is less able to deal with problems of financial exclusion when they reflect social exclusion in situations of structural inequality. Individual disadvantage in such contexts is the product of entrenched social relationship of ethnicity, caste and gender which systematically block the access of certain social groups to market opportunities, government services and the collective forums of decision-making.

A focus on financial services based on commercial

principles, cost recovery and individual lending in such context may very well reinforce social exclusion and exacerbate social inequality.

What is needed instead is a more holistic understanding of the nature of inequality and a more comprehensive approach to tackling it. "Poverty lending" in the way it is characterised by its detractors does not provide this alternative: charity, patronage, welfarism and subsidies have little to offer poor people except the perpetuation of their dependency status. A more viable alternative is represented by organisations which combine financial services with other forms of support and which use group-based strategies to build organisational capacity of the poor. Such organisations are not indifferent to issues of sustainability but define it in terms of the capacity of poor people to sustain themselves over time through integration into mainstream markets and service provision rather than in terms of the capacity of the organisation to reproduce itself over time.

There are, of course, other far more radical approaches to structural change than those associated with microfinance but they may not address the everyday practical needs of the poor as effectively as microfinance. The appeal of microfinance is that it can provide a very practical basis for poor women to come together on a regular basis at the same time as promoting new ideas, opportunities and social relations with the potential to address strategic gender interests. Not all MFOs choose to take on this larger transformative agenda no indeed could they without undermining their roles as efficient providers of financial services.

However, there is no reason why organisations concerned with social transformation cannot co-exist alongside organisations concerned with a narrower financial agenda. Indeed, they may prove complementary or synergistic in their effects. In my study of Nijera Kori in Bangladesh, for instance, I found that its members were also often members of Grameen Bank, thus having to attend who sets of meeting a week [Kabeer 2003, 2005]. However, they valued their membership of both organisations for different reasons. They valued Grameen Bank because it provided them with access to "usefully large" sums of money when they needed it while they valued their association with Nijera Kori because it helped them stand up for themselves.

Similarly, in my study of SEDP, a women explained the difference between the training she had received from Saptagram, an explicitly feminist organisation for landless women, and from SEDP, an organisation for promoting small enterprise: "Before I joined Saptagram, you could say I was stupid...I was like a child. Saptagram taught me to think for myself. With SEDP training, I also learnt something new, how to do business. Which is better? Both are important" [Kabeer 2001: 79].

Conclusion

The findings reviewed in this paper suggest the need for caution in talking about the impact of microfinance, in general, and the need to talk about the impact particular organisations have had in particular contexts. MFOs vary considerably in the contexts in which they work, the sections of the population they work with, their analysis of the problem of financial exclusion, the strategies they adopt to address this problem and the commitment they bring to bear in the implementation of their strategies. Organisations with apparently similar approaches may nevertheless report very different benefits because of variation in some of these factors.

However, regardless of the pace and the extent of the change that they bring about, the review in this paper suggests that microfinance offers an important and effective means to achieving change on a number of different fronts, economic, social and perhaps also political. The success of MFOs in building up the organisational capacity of poor women provides the basis for their social mabilisation that many other development interventions have not been able to achieve. Indeed, their very success may be their undoing: there is growing unease at the way in which both governments and populist political parties may be seeking to capitalise on the idea of self-help groups for their own instrumental purposes.

An important question that remains unanswered relates to the longer term impact of microfinance. We noted that there was very little evidence relating to the extent to which microfinance clients graduated out of poverty and into mainstream financial services. To some extent, these reflect the fact that there are very few longitudinal studies which track clients over a sufficient period of time to be able to tell us how they fared. There is clearly a need for microfinance organisations to develop some time frame within which they would expect to see tangible results.

But it may reflect the limits to microfinance as a

tool for poverty reduction. However effective the role of microfinance organisations in providing financial services to the poor, they cannot substitute for broader policies to promote pro-poor economic growth, equitable social development and democratic participation in collective forums of decision-making. In the absence of such policies, microfinance may at most provide a safety net for the poor rather than a ladder out of poverty.

And finally, to return to the question with which we started the paper, it is clear that while access to financial services can and does make important contributions to the economic productivity and social well-being of poor women and their households, it does not "automatically" empower women—any more than do education, political quotas, access to waged work or any of the other interventions that feature in the literature on women's empowerment. There are no magic bullets, no panaceas, no blueprints, no readymade formulas which bring about the radical structural transformation that the empowerment of the poor, and of poor women, implies. These various interventions are simply different entry points into this larger project, each with the potential for social transformation, but each contingent on context, commitment and capacity if this potential is to be realized.

4

Equality of Gender Indicators and Poverty Reduction

South Asia hosts the largest numbers of the world's poor. Although various poverty-measuring indicators have been used in different times, by all indicators, poverty in south Asia is acute and also wide in magnitude. Of the five south Asian countries, Sri Lanka seems much better both in terms of income poverty and human poverty, but others lag far behind (Table 1).

According to World Bank's one dollar-a-day income-poverty line, out of 1.3 billion poor people in the world, 40 per cent (515 million) live in south Asia, even though the region accounted for only 23 per cent of the global population (South Asia HDR 2000:13). Income disparities in south Asia were one of the largest in the world, the richest 10 per cent being more than six times as wealthy as the poorest 10 per cent.

Similarly south Asia lags far behind even other

developing countries on Human Development and Gender Development Indices (Table 3).

Taking account of such a situation, the governments and the UN agencies have set poverty reduction as their main agenda in the region. Given the pervasive formal and informal social, economic and political exclusion of women in the region and the impact this has on women's poverty, gender equality through mainstreaming at policy and increasingly at programme levels has acquired special importance in their agenda.

Defining Poverty, Exclusion and Empowerment

Poverty is a state of being, whereby people lack: *(a)* income and assets to obtain basic necessities, *(b)* voice and power in the institutions of state and society, *(c)* freedoms and a level playing field to live their levels on basic of equality and justice, and *(d)* are vulnerable to adverse shocks and unable to cope with them. In this context, poverty may be defined in a three-dimensional perspective, economic, human and environmental. There is now general recognition that effective poverty reduction requires not only income growth but also improved human capabilities and efficient use of resources.

Economic or income poverty includes extreme or absolute poverty, defined as lack of income necessary to satisfy basic needs, food usually defined on the basis of minimum calorie requirements, clothing and shelter. Relative poverty, defined as lack of income necessary to satisfy culturally determined minimum standards of living.

Environmental and ecological poverty includes

degraded land, lack of clean air and water, inadequate access to natural resources, and lack of basic physical infrastructure necessary to sustain basic human capabilities, to increase the accessibility of goods and services and to face natural disasters, typhoons, floods, landslides, etc.

Human poverty includes absence or reduced capabilities such as illiteracy, malnutrition, an abbreviated life span, poor maternal health, lack of access to services and morbidity and death from preventable diseases. Following Amartya Sen, human poverty is now understood to include lack of rights and freedoms that enable people to realize their full potential and a lack of voice in the governance process. Successive editions of the UNDP's Human Development Report have stressed people centered development. Concepts of exclusion and inclusion acquire specific importance in this context.

Table 1: Poverty Profile of Selected South Asian Countries

Country	*Per Cent Population below Income Poverty Line $ 1 a Day*		*Human Poverty Index (HPI)*	*Poverty of Opportunity Index (POPI)*
	(1989-94)	*(1990-2002)*	*(1995)*	*(2004)*
Pakistan	12	13.4	41.9	44
Nepal	53	37.7	41.2	52
Bangladesh	29	36.0	42.2	46
India	53	34.7	31.4	38
Sri Lanka	4	6.6	18.2	27

Source: Human Development in South Asia 2000: 12 and Human Development Report 2004: 147-49.

Table 2: Per Capita PPP and Income Distribution in Selected SAARC Countries

Country	*PPP $*		*Per Cent of the Income*	
	Male	*Female*	*Top 10*	*Bottom 10*
Bangladesh	2035	1150	26.7	3.9
India	3820	1442	27.4	3.9
Nepal	1776	891	29.8	3.2
Pakistan	2789	915	28.3	3.7
Sri Lanka	4523	2570	28.0	3.5

Source: HDR, 2004; data for other SAARC countries not available.

Thus exclusion, poverty and gender overlap in many ways, but not completely. Although women and certain castes are discriminated against on the basis of gender and caste, neither are all women poor nor all people on the excluded group, are poor. Poverty, gender and exclusion may be visualised in terms of three partly overlapping circles. Each circle is larger than the overlapping parts, but reinforcing each other manifold within the overlapping part.

Exclusion

In no country the population is entirely homogeneous. The world's nearly 200 countries contain some 5,000 ethnic groups [UNDP 2004:2]. In south Asia, in addition to religious and racial diversity the entrenched caste system further discriminates against various groups. Often exclusion is multidimensional—economic, social, cultural, geographic, rural and each aspect reinforces the other. Economic exclusion is measured through poverty (percentage of people below poverty line), income disparity, wage differentials, and access and control over productive resources (land, credit, enterprise, capital, and technology), access to housing, level of employment, etc.

Social/cultural exclusion centres on caste hierarchies, ethnicity, religion, class stratification, sexual orientation, marital status, individual status in the family, etc. The Human Development Report 2004 identifies two forms of cultural exclusion as:

Participation exclusion: The cultural exclusion of a person groups may sometimes take the form of not allowing the person or group to participate in society in the way others are allowed and encouraged to do due to their cultural affiliation or gender. In south Asian countries mainly women, poor and so called low-caste people are excluded from the participation in many social-economic and political decision-making processes by saying that they are ignorant, uneducated and unwilling to participate.

Living modes of exclusion: It denies recognition of a lifestyle that an individual or group may choose to have. And this intolerance can go with the insistence that members of the group must live exactly like others in the society. Such exclusion is based on religious intolerance and discriminatory treatment to widows, lesbians and gays, immigrants, and the so-called lower castes. Blatant discrimination against widows in upper caste Hindu culture, especially in Nepal and in India is a mixture of both participation and living modes of exclusion.

Similarly exclusion could be formal as well as informal. Formally, there may still be laws, which discriminate against women and various groups of people. For example, in Nepal, 54 laws and 185clauses/ section/rules/schedules/annexes discriminate against them [FWLD 2000]. In Pakistan, many Islamic laws discriminate against women. On the other hand, there may be legal equality as in the case of dalits in Nepal and harijans in India, but they could be still discriminated in practice. Bhattachan et al (2003) have recorded 205 such practices against dalits, although legally caste discrimination was abolished in 1956. Such formal and informal exclusion present most formidable barriers to human development and must be removed by the process of empowerment. Since poverty is a result of as much a lack of voice and power as of material resources, empowerment of women and other disadvantaged groups is a precondition to breaking the vicious circle of poverty and voiceless status.

Empowerment

Empowerment is an ongoing and dynamic process, which enhances women's and any other marginalized and alienated groups' abilities to change the structures and ideologies that keep them subordinate. It is a process of making present power structures more inclusive, including all women and men, senior citizens, dalits, indigenous people and people with disabilities [Bhasin and Dhar 1998], Empowerment is therefore clearly concerned with power, and particularly with the power relations—and distribution of power-between individuals and groups [Kahlon 2004, S. Batliwala 1994: 17].

In the current context, the Nepal Human Development Report (2004:12) views empowerment as a process-and also as the result of the process – whereby the powerless or less powerful members of society and the women gain greater access and control over material and intellectual resources, and challenge the ideologies of discrimination and subordination, which justify this unequal distribution.

The final goal of empowerment is to transform the ideology and practice of domination and subordination, challenge and transfer existing power structures, systems and institutions which have upheld and reinforced this discrimination and gained access to and control over material and knowledge resources. Empowerment and inclusion are often seen as complementary processes, empowerment focusing on enhancing the various capabilities of the excluded groups "from above" create enabling environment at the systems level for the excluded groups to enjoy their rights [SFID/World Bank 2005:8].

A combination of these two complementary processes is needed to enhance human capabilities, voice and agency role of women and other disadvantaged and alienated groups. Combining the two, the South Asian Women's meeting in 1998, laid out several points as components of women's empowerment. The empowerment process may be broken down in three dimensions, economic, social and political, which reinforce each other, While the economic aspects would include increasing women's access to, and command over tangible and intangible resources, such as wealth, property, employment, knowledge and information, social aspect would include changing the existing discriminatory ideology and culture, which determine the environment for women's existence. Finally, political process must increase women's presence and influence in the power structure. Political ability to bring about changes in women's legal status, to direct resources to women, and to get access to positions of power is of crucial importance. Each component reinforces the other. Viewing empowerment as a process, these processes should occur simultaneously but different groups can be at different stages.

Table 3: Human Development Indicators

Country	*Per Cent Adults Literate*		*Per Cent Enrolled (Gross in (Primary + Secondary + Tertiary))*		*Life Expectancy (years)*		*HDI Value*	*GDI Value*
	Male	*Female*	*Male*	*Female*	*Male*	*Female*		
Bangladesh	50.3	31.4	53	54	60.7	61.5	0.509	0.499
Bhutan	-	-	-	-	61.8	64.3	0.536	-
India	69.0	46.4	62	48	63.1	64.4	0.595	0.572
Maldives	97.3	97.2	78	78	67.7	66.8	0.752	-
Nepal	61.6	26.4	67	55	59.9	59.4	0.504	0.484
Pakistan	53.4	28.5	43	31	61.0	60.7	0.497	0.471
Sri Lanka	94.7	89.6	64	66	69.8	75.8	0.740	0.738
SAARC	71.0	53.2	61.3	55.3	63.4	64.7	0.590	0.552

Source: Human Development Report 2004.

Moreover, the understanding of political power must be broadened to include, besides the access to basic needs and services, freedom and ability to: *(a)* make decisions about their own life options, for example, marry not to marry, when, where and how such to study/work, where to live, etc, *(b)* make others implement one's decision and, *(c)* to influence decisions about others in the household, community, nation and international arena at large [Batliwala 1994].

Measurement and Indicators

The first step towards ensuring empowerment and inclusion of the excluded women and men is making the disparities visible. In the last two decades or so, a great deal of thought has gone into now to measure this multidimensional nature of poverty, gender status and empowerment. Starting with the introduction of Human Development Index (HDI) in Human Development Report (HDR) in 1990, successive HDRs have tried to improve and supplement this indicator with other indicators. The HDI is a composite index of relative income, life expectancy, and education attainments on global scale. Similarly Gender Development Index (GDI), introduced since 1994, measures women's achievement on a similar scale relative to men on a global scale.

A multidimensional measures of poverty introduced in the Human Development Report 1997, is a reverse image of the HDI, Human Poverty Index (HPI) that focuses on human deprivation instead of human achievements. It brings together in one composite index the deprivation in four basic dimensions of human life [Nepal Human Development Report 2004:119]: *(i)* Inability to live a long and healthy life, measured by the percentage of people born alive today not expected to survive to age 40; *(ii)* knowledge, measured by the adult illiteracy rate; *(iii)* economy provisioning, per cent people without access to safe water and percentage of malnourished children under age five; and *(iv)* social exclusion.

Another similar measure in use is the Poverty of Opportunity Index (POPI), development by Mahbub ul Haq Foundation, that adds an income component of human deprivation in addition to factors which are included in HPI.

Much development has also taken place in the evolution of macro-level indicators on women's status in the last three decades. Firstly, CEDAW and various international conventions and agreements have provided a benchmark for measuring women's legal (formal and informal) discriminatory structures and disparities visible. The focus on sex disaggregated information and data has yielding useful tools for analysis. The UN system's definitions of production. Economic activity rates and the informal-sector work have improved much from the earlier pre-1993 manual on the System of National Accounts [UN et al 1993]. In the new manual, any activity, which others can do for oneself is defined as work ("Any activity that contributes to the production of goods and services within the production boundary", [UN et al 1993]).

However, still only all products for commercial exchange and marketed services are now within the System of National Accounts (SNA). The household maintenance and children are still not considered service and outside SNA [Acharya 2000; Beneria 2003].

It should be noted that just sex-disaggregated data is not adequate for gender analysis. Gender indicators must reflect women's realities. For example in many countries sex-disaggregated or not, economic activity data do not reflect such realities. Further such data much always be comparative with men and they must be disaggregated by caste/ethnicity/region, urban/ rural, regional.

For a deeper role analysis of the opportunity spectrum they need to be supplemented by measures of *(a)* changes in the structural and ideological inequalities, *(b)* changes in the role within the household or stereotyping and degree of freedom in decisions on her own life and influence over the community matters, national and international decision-making process.

Gender Empowerment Index (GEM) and GDI provide incomplete but useful tools of unified quantitative analysis. But GDI and GMI do not capture the whole socio-economic and political environment of a women's existence. For example GDI contains only market income, besides access to education and life expectancy; the implicit assumption being that wage income is better for women than subsistence work. But the realities in developing countries show that unskilled wage workers are at the bottom of the socio-economic hierarchy. Households would not send their women for wage work, unless poverty forces them to do so. Similarly GEM has an additional flaw of only encompassing women's presence in decision-making positions and not their power's which is a product of all economic, social and political structures as well as ideology.

Making Disparities Visible

Successive human development reports since 1994 have

tried to make gender disparities visible. The 2004 HDR concentrates on making exclusions of various kings visible. The South Asian Human Development Report (2000) has focused on making women's contributions to economic work and the household care in south Asian visible.

It emphasized that a vast majority of south Asian women work in the informal sector or in unpaid family assistance which accounts for 96 per cent economically active women in India, 75 per cent each in Nepal and Bangladesh, and nearly 65 per cent in Pakistan.

Further, in south Asia as around the world, mainly women are responsible for producing and nourishing family members.

Their reproductive role is most valuable for the sustenance of their households, communities, and to the nation. Still it is seriously under-appreciated. Caring labour provided by women within the household is rarely recorded and not socially recognised as work even now, because it is argued that it is impossible to quantify and ascribe an economic value to it [UN et al 1993].

In India, women account for 60 per cent of unpaid family workers (in economic work) and 98 per cent of those, engaged in domestic work [South Asia HDR 2000:56]. In Nepal they constitute 52 per cent of total work force if those engaged solely in household maintenance activities are added to those, who also contribute to economic work also [Acharya 2003]. In terms of the total human hours spent on household work and child care, women contributed 84 per cent (Nepal Labour Force Survey, 1998-1999).

In south Asia invisibility of women's work has been particularly pervasive because of historical, traditional and cultural reasons [South Asia HDR, 2000]. The ideology of seclusion makes women's work outside the household a matter of dishonour, resulting in the under-reporting of women's economic activities. The enumerators own bias compounds the problem.

Some countries in the region, particularly India, Pakistan and Nepal made specific efforts in their 2001 census exercises to eliminate such biases in reporting. UN agencies including UNIFEM facilitated this exercise by funding exchange visits and other activities in each country. In Nepal's in additional to specifically defining and exemplifying some of the work categories and eliminating reporting biases, an effort was made to redefine the category of economic work as per SNA 2001. The category of economic activity in Nepal's case work expended to include procession, collection and gathering of fuel wood, water, etc, and production of immediately non-perishable products (e.g., ghee, pickle, dry foods, mats, wheat, rice and corn flower, etc). Such activities were defined as extended economic activities. People involved in these activities (at least one hour per day) were also considered as economically active. Further in contrast to earlier censuses, where people were defined as economically active or not active on the basis of what they reported, in the 2001 census every body above 10 years was required to report their activities during the reference year. This allowed for classification of people as per what they did, than what the reported. Moreover, the concepts were defined much clearly than in the earlier census. All these measures have contributed to increasing women's economic activity records by about 12 percentage points.

In other countries no such redefinitions were effected. The focus was on probing questions, clarifications and correct reporting. Even with old definitions, women constituted 44 per cent of the economically active population in the region. But it is evident from Table 4 that the data in Pakistan is still more biased than in other countries, reflecting the cultural bias and the prevalent to acceptance of women's seclusion and invisibility, which is an illusory reality because, no household can survive without women's contributions to livelihood, visible or not visible.

Nepal presents an example of making women's total work visible from the census itself [Acharya 2003]. For this a new category of "working population" has been introduced, which combines percentages of both economically active and home-markers. Any person engaged solely in home-making is also considered working. Work is defined as an activity, which a second person can do for you, for example cooking, taking care of children, cleaning, washing, households maintenance and child-care activities. Only activities, which a second person cannot do for you, for example, sleeping, taking care of your own person, watching TV, study, etc, are excluded from the definition of work. By this definition of work. By this definition of work, more than 90 per cent of men and women is the 25-54 age groups are working; the difference is only in the kind of work they do. Among all age cohorts, larger proportions of women perform economic plus extended economic activities than just home-making. Even those who were economically active contribute disproportionately to household maintenance. Acharya (2000) working with 1991 GDP data and time-use survey showed that if women's services in the household were valued even at minimum prices of the products and services, the amount thus generated would be more than the measured GDP.

Besides, a concerted effort was made in the 2001 census to engender the whole process, so that they reflected the actual work patterns of men and women and also living modes. As a consequence women activists have now information on many more aspects of women's lives such as kind of marriage and polygamy, ownership of house, land and animals, living arrangements of children below 16, and education and professional and political access by caste/ethnicity and gender, etc. Such data provide a rich statistical evidence of the impact of discriminatory institutions and practices on various groups of population and women.

Gender activists can now produce statistical proof that polygamy, which is a major cause of domestic violence [New Era 1997], still exists in Nepal, despite a legal ban. There are about 5, 55,000 women living in polygamous marriages. They can now statistically prove that only a small number of women own economic assets, providing a powerful instrument for the advocacy of equal property rights to parental property. Only about 11 per cent households had some landing the women's legal ownership while only about 6 per cent households had some house in women's name [TPAMF 2005]. Overall, only 0.8 per cent of the households had all three, house, land and livestock in women's names against the fact that overall 88 per cent of the households were living in the family owned houses and 76 per cent of the households had some land. Similarly as against 71 per cent of the households having some livestock, only 7 per cent households reported women's livestock ownership, despite multiple credit-institutions targeting and funding this activity for women.

Similarly now they can now counter with statistical evidence, the argument that women do not constitute a specific treatment. Chart 2 extracted from a recent census based study [TPAMF 2005], features an index that combines educational and professional achievements as also representation in the various political, higher administrative and managerial as also judicial decision-making positions by caste/ethnicity. It presents a powerful counter to this thesis. It illustrates that within no group, achievements of women match those of men, except for musahars, where both women and men are at the bottom of the scale, although both women and men of Newar and Brahmin/chhetri and Thakali, the traditionally powerful groups, top the list. However, women of powerful groups do have higher scores than men of many others castes and ethnicities as well. A wider difference between women and men indices among the terai groups in general (10 to 12 points) and hill Brahmin/Chhetris and Thakalis should also be noted. The differences are highest for the hill brahmins, an impact of the ideology of women's seclusion.

Empowerment and Inclusion Indicators

Empowerment perhaps is the most difficult to measure. Currently most commonly used indicators include access to economic resources, education and knowledge, healthcare services and participation in the decision-making processes in the household and political administrative power structures. With emphasis on education, HDI, GDI, GEM and all other indicators are calculated by specific groups as well.

At the marco level, GEM is a useful indicator. It measures gender disparity in political access to decision-making positions in political, administrative and professional fields. It is composed of distances from positions of gender equality, in terms of purchasing partly, income percentages of seats held by women impairments, percentage of women in legislatures, senior officials and mangers among professionals and technical workers. Thus, GEM concentrates on participation, economic, political and professional, while GDI concentrates primarily on basic capabilities and living standards [HDR 1995:82].

However, GEM measures only disparity in earned income and professional and political achievements. But earned income constitutes a very inadequate representation of gender inequality. Similarly presence is only a precondition of real empowerment. Much deeper role analysis is needed to measure whether the structural and ideological inequities are changing to empower women in a real sense. Further their role within the household and changes in the opportunity spectrum must also be reflected in future empowerment indices.

Using Macro-level Variables

Developing indicators to measure ideological changes and translating available macro-level indicators for impact analysis of programmes and projects is a complex task, which the full paper deals in some detail with examples from south Asia. Two points to note at the outset are that any set of indicators used for measuring progress towards gender equality must capture the process of change in women's opportunity spectrum" in totality, economic, social and political. It is understood that changes in the social environment is a long-drawn out process. But the programmes/ projects must also be evaluated in terms of whether they contribute positively to progress towards equality or reinforce the existing inequities.

Some of the indicators of empowerment, which are now drawing international attention and have partly become a regular part of impact analysis include access and rights to resources and economic opportunities and information (land, jobs, education, knowledge, health services, etc.), the division of labour and work load, access to services and institutions that supply them, involvement in household decision-making, political awareness and interest (voting, decisions about voting and relative representation in public decision-making bodies at community, state and national levels) (see for example HDR, 2004).

Besides, the above indicators, which are primarily based on access and presence, additional indicators are needed to measure the voice of women and the excluded and the effectiveness of this "voice" in the power structure, within the household, in the community, in the state and in the state and in interstate institutions and power structure. Such indicators must measure the ability of women and the excluded to make decisions about themselves, to put forward their perspective/vision, to convince others, influence the decisions of others and lead.

Table 4: Selected indicators on Economic Activity Rates in SAARC Region (15+ years)

Country	*Women's Economic Activity Rates*	*Women's Economic Activity Rates as Per Cent of Men's Economic Activity Rates*
Bangladesh	66.4	76
Bhutan	57.1	65
India	42.4	50
Maldives	65.4	80
Nepal	56.8	67
Pakistan	36.3	44
Sri Lanka	43.3	56
South Asia	43.7	52

Source: Human Development Report 2004: 230-232.

Before venturing into a discussion of indicators, a few points need to be noted in this context. All policies enunciated by the programmes or projects on resource transfer, pricing and subsidies as well as decision-making structures, institutions and implementation mechanisms must be seen through a gender perspective at the very beginning of the programme/project. This process must form an integral part of the main body of the programme/project and not as an afterthought in the appendix. Without such an exercise gender concerns often get lost somewhere along the line.

Through Gender Lenses

Pricing and subsidy policies incorporated in projects should also assess the magnitude of their likely impact on a gender and envisage remedial measures. In recent years under structural adjustment programmes, projects are debarred for provisioning of agricultural subsidies, without examining their impact on women and the poor in specific situations. Such a blanket ban has often resulted in further excluding the excluded from the availability services and facilities and worsening the situation of women.

Goals set for engendering component or women's projects should be broad enough to cater for major needs of women and other disadvantaged groups as equal participants and not as marginals. Mainstreaming should not be interpreted to mean adding small components for women in mega projects, specially in agriculture and forestry, where women are the primary workers.

Such an approach may require a change in the whole thinking process—from designing projects for men with little components for women, to designing projects for women with small components for men where necessary. For example, in forestry, environment-related and irrigation projects, any resettlement areas ownership or user rights to households could be granted through women. This could go a long way in correcting property rights in south Asia, which are already heavily skewed against women. In rural infrastructure and industrial sectors, projects should provide for equal opportunities to women in employment, for skill and management training for conventional and non-conventional activities.

Additionally the industries sectors, the projects should ensure opportunities and extend credit to women to acquire shares when public enterprises are being privatised and shares are being allotted to the workers. The working environment in terms of ventilation, sanitation and hygiene, childcare, hostel facilities and security issues should address women's concerns, programme/projects must ensure adequate financial resources for the gender aspect and allocate adequate resources to counter structural and ideological exclusion at the practical level.

Promoting women's agency for programme/project efficiency and benefit sharing is not enough; programmes must address the context and ideology of male supremacy. For example, dalit women are likely to be excluded from jobs in project-funded hotel and catering business or drinking water facilities, unless specific efforts are made to include them. Microcredit projects should start integrating more comprehensive gender training to communities as a whole. It has been clearly indicated by many studies [Acharya 1989; ADB 1997; Fisher et al 2002; Goetz 2001] that only those microcredit projects with components of social transformation have long-term empowering impact on women. Recognising women's agency for better credit management without attempts to change the context and ideology of male supremacy at a broader level can have only limited impact on social transformation.

The implementation machinery must be sensitive to both gender and exclusion issues, including in the programme planning, budgeting, implementation, monitoring and evaluation, user groups and community resource management committees. Women's role in the decision-making process may be measured firstly by whether there are women in decision-making process may be measured firstly by whether there are women in decision-making positions or not . But this is not adequate to measure her role in the process. Her gender attitude as also the gender attitude of the whole programmed/projects implementing agencies must be gender-friendly.

Monitoring of gender aspects must be sufficiently integrated in the regular monitoring/evaluation processes and the process supervision at all levels. Separate gender analysis in the annex could be a necessary component but it is not sufficient for regular monitoring of the programme. Not only the inputs gut processes, outcomes and impacts (where possible) must be monitored throughout the programme/project implementation period. Incorporation of gender is required at all points where process. Beneficiary or/ and participation is involved. All project monitoring and supervision documentation should cover gender aspects when monitoring income, employment, beneficiary participation and other process indicators.

Monitoring Indicators

The discussions above point to a wide spectrum of available indicators for poverty, human development and empowerment. Our task should be to convert all these macro-level indicators into a set of variables, which could be used in a development impact evaluation framework to assess programmes and projects from a gender and inclusion perspectives. The main point is to capture the process of change in the opportunity structure and life options. It is understood that changes in the social environment is a long-drawn out process. But the programmes/projects must also be evaluated in terms of whether they contribute positively to progress towards equality or reinforce the existing inequities.

First of all, all information on employment, income, land ownership, beneficiary participation, staff and other training, access to services such as extension, health and education must be broken down by gender at all stages of the project cycle.

It would be useful to separate outcome and impact indicators for monitoring. Impact analysis must capture not only outcomes but also gender impacts at the intra-households level and social implications resulting from project activities. In Table 5 some indicative examples are presented for agricultural extension, microcredit, community forestry and rural infrastructure. Some of the variables which are usually classified under impact (such as employment and income) are classified under outcome in the example presented. This is required because: *(a)* where project inputs are directed to households, the intra-household allocation of income and project benefits cannot be clearly captured by regular household level indicators of income, employment, etc. Specific efforts should be made to evaluate the impact on the intra-household distribution of resources and division of labour, and *(b)* social life is complex and just employment and income are not adequate to study social processes. All such information should be broken down by caste/class/ethnicity/indigenous people, etc.

Table 5: Some Indicators of Impact on Gender

Outcome

Agricultural Extension

(a) Number of women/men extension staff trained and recruited.

(b) Number of women/men farmer contacted.

(c) Inputs supplied to women's/men's crops (where this division is visible).

(d) Research trails carried out for women's/men's crops (when this division exists).

(e) New technology diffused for women specific/men's crops (when this division exists)

(f) New technology diffused for women specific /men specific operations.

Community Forestry

(a) Land area allocated to women/men groups.

(b) Trees planted.

(c) Women's and men's groups organised and trained. Number of women/men participants in joint groups.

(d) Seedling distributed to women's/men's groups.

(e) Extension messages diffused to women/men.

(f) Women/men staff trained.

Micro credit

(a) Number trained and volume of credit given to women/ men.

(b) Women's/men's employment rate/income

(c) Women/men staff trained.

Rural Infrastructure

(a) Roads in km completed.

(b) Buildings constructed – square meters allocated women, where relevant to childcare and sanitation facilities for women.

(c) Employment generated for women and men.

(d) Women and men (staff and workers) trained.

Impact
Agricultural Extension
(a) Change in farming practices of women's/men's crops/operations.
(b) Change in productivity of women's/men's crops/operation.
(c) Income changes for women and men-headed households.
(d) Number of women/men getting or losing land because of land price increase.
(e) Number of women/men gaining/losing employment because of new technology.
(f) Numbers of women/men displaced from operations, learning technology, or getting new employment.
(g) Women's/men's workloads and wage rates.
Community Forestry
(a) Area of forest protected and planted.
(b) Environmental cleanliness.
(c) Increased flow of water.
(d) Time required for collecting fuel and water.
(e) Women's command over the forest area, output and income from the forestry.
Microcredit
(a) Increase in women's command over income.
(b) Self-respect and awareness.
(c) Decision-making role within the household and in the community/voting rate.
(d) Women's workload.
Rural Infrastructure
(a) Travel time to market and number of traveller women and men.
(b) New employment and income earning opportunities generated for women and men.
(c) Number of marginal farmers women/men losing/acquiring land-access of women-headed households?
(d) Use of market space by women and men—pre-project and post-project.

Source: Acharya 1997.

Outcomes should be monitored throughout the project implementation period and on completion. In some projects such as microcredit, impact also may be monitored during implementation. In others such as roads, impact evaluation will have to wait until the completion of the project or at least part of the project, but women's involvement in the process should be monitored throughout. Both outcome and impact indicators must be specified clearly in all programs and projects.

Indicators of Impact on Gender Relations

Ultimately, the impact of development on gender must be measured in terms of changes in life options for women. Life options for women are determined not only by material assistance provided directly by the project but by the overall gender ideology and socio-economic structures. Such changes in gender ideology are most important for the success of programme/ project effectiveness. Therefore, social advancement towards gender equality must form an important plank of all programmes, and progress towards it must be recorded and measured. Even if such changes are only limited in the short term, direction of the change must be measured to ensure that at least the programmes have moved in the right direction. Gender relations may be examined under various rubrics. Access to resources and economic opportunities: The first would involve looking at a woman's opportunity structure to work and live where she would like to. As discussed above these are determined both by structural and ideological factors. The first set of indicators therefore, must measure structural factors. These would include formal and informal institutions that determine her access and rights to economic and technology resources, such as economic asset (including land), income earning opportunities and incomes, technology, education and information, health services, etc. These indicators are measurable and used regularly in specific sector level analysis. However, these can be measured and analysed at programme/project level in all kind of programmes, with social mobilisation components.

Impact on the division of labour and workload: How has the ideology and practice of women's exclusive responsibility of the care economy and scope to choose work patterns changed as a result of programme input? Or has it only added to women's workload? A properly designed but quick time-use survey must form an integral part of base line surveys and impact monitoring.

Political power should be understood to encompass power both in the private and public arena. In the private arena, increased self decision-making capacity especially in the choice of education fields, ability to get treatment when sick, and decision to choose their marriage partners and when to marry must form an important part of the indicators for measuring changes in the patriarchal ideology of male domination and women's subordination. Further women's influence over, all decisions in the household about others should also be measured.

Household decisions and women's role in them: The indicator should cover all kinds of decisions made in the household in the reference period. Such decisions could be classified in various ways and recorded as a process. A few points should be noted in this connection. Decisions must be recorded as a process. Second, the questions must cover different time length for different kinds of decisions and third, they must be designed to fit specific cultural issues, besides women's role in farm or economic decisions, as in actual practiced. Further, the whole idea that whether you made the decision by yourself seems too individualistic, specially for south Asia. Therefore, the crucial issues are whether women can influence the decisions effectively. That seems more natural.

Decision-making in the public arena and their effectiveness: just looking at household level decision-making is not adequate. Therefore, women's relative role in public decision-making at various levels, community, state and nation must also be examined. Such participation indicators could be many. Has her freedom to participate in community organisations (health club, library, saving-credit cooperatives, banking, etc.) increased? Has her ability to put forward own perspective/vision to take the leading role in making her own decisions increased? Has her political awareness and interest been enhanced?

The issue is how to measure whether women have been able to effectively influence such decisions. Methods could be devised to record the public process of decision-making as in the case of the households. Some questions are listed in Table 6., How many decisions were made in the community? Whether women agreed to all such decisions and if not why not? What they did to change them? Were they able to change them, etc? Such indicators will vary as per cultural traditions of the community but evaluation of this aspect must be an integral part of the programme/project impact evaluation.

Table 6: Selected Indicators for Measuring Impact on Gender Relations

Economic indicators

(i) Access and rights to resources and opportunities and information structural factors—land, jobs, education, knowledge, health services, etc.

(ii) Impact on the division of labour, workload and time use.

Political indicators

(i) Involvement in household decision-making, ability to influence household decisions.

(ii) Political awareness and interest—voting, decisions about voting, etc.

(iii) Relative participation and voice in public decision-making—community, state and nation.

(iv) Capability to put forward one's own perspective/vision, to convince others and have a voice in the public decision making particularly at the grassroot level.

Social indicators

(i) Freedom to participate in community identifying freedom organizations coercion and violence

(ii) Go where and when one wants to.

(iii) Take membership in various organisations

(iv) Marry as and when one wants to.

(v) Live free from various kinds of violence.

Cultural indicators

(i) To take appropriate action against any forms of discrimination, abuse and violence.

(ii) Be consulted and influence decisions about her own future.

(iii) To voice her grievances against excessive workload and change the stereotypical division of labour.

Inclusion indicators

(i) Participation of these groups in programme and at various decision-makings levels.

(ii) Effectiveness of their voices.

(iii) Benefits from the programme/project.

(iv) Ability to speak out against injustice and claim their rights.

Finally, the ideology of exclusion on the basis of gender: As regards the social aspect, a third set of indicators must measure a women's freedom from coercion and violence? This can overlap very much with political issues. Some questions to be asked could include questions on the increase or decrease in the degree of freedom and ability to get justice, to go where and when she wants to, to secure membership in various organisation, to marry as and when she wants to and live free from various kinds of violence (physical, mental, psychological) inside and outside the household? Are they able to have a voice in the decisions about the future of their own children- their marriage or education, to choose their own career, outside the gender division of labour? Questions need to be devised to fit each specific social situation and culture. Nevertheless, they must be able to capture the progress towards gender equality in socio/cultural ideology as well.

How inclusive the programme has been? Have traditionally excluded groups (for, example dalits in Nepal, harijans in India and Hindus in Pakistan) in the programme areas been included in terms of numbers and effectiveness of participation, benefit-sharing on the basis of equity, their empowerment to speak out against injustice and claim their rights in various services—education, health, access to drinking and irrigation water, etc? How much has the programme been also to remove living modes of exclusions and intolerance in some behavioural patterns, for example, against the widows in Hindu communities, excluded castes/indigenous people and religious minorities and dalits in south Asia in general?

Conclusion

The coverage of indicators used for any programme/project analysis must be broader than what are currently used, so as to capture the whole context of women's existence, political, economic and social aspects, in a local, national as well as in global perspective. Usually advocated and used access and presence-based indicators must be supplemented by new ones to measure changes in a women's life options, the changes in sharing of power and progress towards an equitable society. Indicators for measuring women's power-sharing level must include her freedoms and ability to influence the decisions about her and others at all levels. As to who wields the real power depends not only on economic and political structure but also on social ideology must also be measured. Although these are long-term goals and specific instruments must be designed and used to fit each specific culture, each and every programme/project must contribute positively towards this goal and such contributions should be measured. Likewise, in today's globalizing world, all these indicators must take account of the international power structure as well, in terms of assessing their gender inclusiveness.

Annexure: Per Cent Caste/Ethnic Composition of the Population, Nepal 2001

(In per cent)

Caste Hindus		(57.5 per cent)
	High	(32.8 per cent)
A	Hill/terai B/C+ (a^1+a^2)	32.8
a^1	Hill B/C+ (1+2)	30.9
	1 Brahman (Hill)	12.7
	2 Chhetri, thakuri, sanyasi	18.1
a^2	Terai B/C+ -	1.9
	3 Brahman (terai), rajput, Kayastha, baniya, marwadi, jaine, nurang, bengali	1.9
	Middle	(12.9 per cent)
B	Terai middle castes (include 4-7)	12.9
	4 Yadav	3.9
	5 Teli, kalwar, sudhi, sonar, lohar	3.2
	6 Koiri, kurmi, kanu, haluwi, hajam/thakur, badhe, bahae, rajbhar	3.6
	7 Kewat, Mallah, nuniya, kumhar, kahar, lodha bing/banda, bhediyar, mali, kamar, Dhunia	2.2
	Dalits	(11.8 per cent)
C	Dalits (c^1+c^2)	11.8
C^1	Hill dalits (8-11)	7.1
	8 Kami	3.9
	9 Damai	1.7
	10 Sarki	1.4
	11 Gaine, badi	0.0
C^2	Terai dalits: (12-15)	4.7
	12 Chamar	1.2
	13 Musahar	0.8
	14 Dhusadh/paswan, tatma, khatway, bantar, dom, chidimar	1.6
	15 Dhobi, halalkhor, dalit/unidentified dalit 0.7	
Janajati		(32.2 per cent)
	Newar and thakali	(5.5 per cent)
D	Janajatis (d^1+d^2)	
d^1	Hill janajatis ($d^{1.1}$+$d^1.d^2$)	37.2
d^{11}	Newar/thakali (16+17)	5.5
	16 Newar	5.5

17 Thakali	0.1
Other hill janajatis	(23 per cent)
D[1.2] other hill janajatis (18-28)	
18 Magar	23.0
19 Tamang	7.1
20 Rai	5.6
21 Gurung	2.8
22 Limbu	2.4
23 Sherpa	1.6
24 Bhote, Walung, Byansi, Hyolmo	0.7
25 Gharti/Bhujel, Kumal, Sunuwar, Baramu, Pahari, adivasi janajati	0.1
26 Yakkha, Chantal, Jirel, Darai, Dura	1.5
27 Majhi, Danuwar, Thami, Lepcha 0.2	
28 Chepang, Bote, Raji, Hayu, Raute, Kusunda	0.7
Terai janajatis (8.7 per cent)	
d.2 Terai janajatis (29-32)	
29 Tharu	8.7
30 Dhanuk	6.7
31 Rajbanshi, Tajpuiya, Gangai, Dhimal, Meche, Kesan, Munda	0.7
32 Santha/Satar, Dhangad/Jhangad, Koche, Pattarkatta/Kusbadiya	0.4
Religious minorities and others	(5.3 per cent)
E Religious minorities	4.3
33 Muslim, churoute	4.3
34 Panjabi/shikh	0.0
35 Unidentified/others	1.0
Total	100

Human Security and Gender Violence

The Commission on Human Security, a product of the 2000 UN Millennium Summit, defined human security as "protecting fundamental freedoms—freedoms that are the essence of life. It means protecting people from critical (serve) and pervasive (widespread) threats and situations. It means using processes that build on people's strengths and aspirations. It means creating political, social, environmental, economic, military and cultural systems that together give people the building blocks of survival, livelihood and dignity.

How a society confronts the issue of violence against women goes to the heart of how women experience security. Freedom from violence and the threat of violence is the first measurement of women's capacity for survival and empowerment. The United Nations Declaration on the Elimination of Violence Against Women states in its preamble that violence, it is this his economic, military and cultural systems that together give people the building blocks of survival, livelihood and dignity.

How a society confronts the issue of violence against women goes to the heart of how women experience security. Freedom from violence and the threat of violence is the first measurement of women's capacity for survival and empowerment. The United Nations Declaration on the Elimination of Violence Against Women states in its preamble that violence against women is a product of the "unequal power relations" that characterize gender relationships in all parts of the world. The declaration recognizes that in addition to individual acts of violence, it is this history of unequal relationships that is at the core of widespread and pervasive nature of violence against women. Violence against women is a universal reality but at the same time it is invisible. Yet such violence is under-reported if not "normalised" as acceptable social behaviour. South Asia has been classified as the worst region in terms of indicators with the highest rates of different forms of violence against women [UNICEF 2001].

The historically unequal power relations between

men and women have been manifested in a variety of ways. As the first report of the UN Special Rapporteur on Violence Against Women states, "the system of male domination has historical roots and is functions and manifestations change over time. The oppression of women is therefore a question of politics, requiring an analysis of the institutions of state and society, the conditioning and socialization of individuals, and the nature of economic and social exploitation" [Report of Special Rapporteur on Vaw 1995]. Recognising the important role that states can play in transforming legislative, administrative and judicial practices , the report points to the fact that states are nevertheless also perpetrators of violence against women whether in prisons, jails or during armed conflict and when turning a blind eye to violence against women that takes place in their society.

Economic and social exploitation of women and their labour also contributes to violence against women. Women are often employed as bonded labour and as low paid labour in many economic enterprises around the world; as migrant workers they face enormous hardship. The refusal to recognise women's economic independence and empowerment is one of the main reasons for violence against women, accentuating thereby, their vulnerability and abuse.

Violence against women also takes place in the most intimate of places, the family. Though the family is often a site of nature and care, it can also be a place where male power is brutally expressed and where women are socialized to accept their inferiority and vulnerability. It is the family that often first teachers women to have negative, disempowering self-images and it is in the family that young men first learn about female subordination.

As the special rapporteur writes, in the context of power relations, it is also men who control the knowledge systems of the world. Whether it is science and modern technology, or religion and its edicts, women are often excluded from creating symbolic systems or analyzing and transmitting knowledge. In these systems of knowledge, women's experience is devalued and privatised and the public world becomes the site of the struggle for power and the vindication of rights. The public private distinction relegates women to the sphere of domestic activity, immune from scrutiny and activism, while men control and determine public power and the priorities of a society as a whole.

Recommendation 19 of Convention on the Elimination of Violence Against Women (CEDAW) and the United Nations Declaration on Violence Against Women calls on states to take immediate steps with regard to ending gender-based violence in the family, in the community and by the state. They call on the states to enact national plans of action, to train and sensitise their criminal justice systems, to provide social support to the victim/survivors and to collect data and information of violence against women in their societies. In a survey conducted by the office of the UN Special Rapporteur on Violence Against Women in 2003, except for a handful of countries most countries had taken some measures with regard to eradicating violence against women. Countries had begun to enact or reform laws that related to training and sensitising their criminal justice systems and had begun running campaigns to prevent violence against women. Some had also adopted social programmes in partnership with NGOs for the women victims.

These newly emerging international norms and standards are still very aspirational in content. The reality on the ground has not changed dramatically. The WHO's report on Violence and Health (2002) still points to widespread violence against women in all parts of the globe, and many parts of the world where women victims of violence accepted violence as an ordinary part of their lives. In all studies, south Asia continues to be a region where violence against women in prevalent, some say even "normalised" as an accepted pattern of behaviour.

Forms of Violence

South Asia has particular cultural and religious practices that also accentuate the problem of VAW in the region. The general low status of women in the region and the entrenched nature of discriminatory structures have let to what is seen as a "lifecycle of VAW" Even before birth women suffer from sex selective abortion, at infancy they may face female infanticide, as young children they will have to put up with incest and son preference, as adolescents they may be sex abused or trafficked, as young women they may suffer rape, sexual harassment, acid attacks; as wives they may experience domestic violence, dowry related violence, marital rape or honour killings, and as widows they may be required to self immolate or be deprived of property and dignity. The vulnerability to violence at every stage of the lifecycle makes VAW a terrible south Asian legacy that requires concerted regional, national and local level action.

Armed Conflict

Rani lives in the east coast of Sri Lanka. Rani is a Sri Lankan Tamil. Rani's husband was taken away by the Sri Lankan army about fifteen years ago and she has not heard from him since. Her son, who was still a child of 12, was taken by the Liberation Tigers of Sri Lanka. She has lost touch with him and does not know whether he is dead or alive. Rani and her daughter eke out a living doing handicrafts with the help of a local NGO. They barely have enough to survive. Her daughter suffers from nightmares and depression since she was attached to both the father and the brother. Rani doesn't like to speak much—speech is dangerous in the east coast with so many young men with guns. Tears swell in her eyes when she speaks. For solace she goes to the nearby oracle to find out about her husband and her son. The oracle tells her that they are alive so she lives in hope (author's notes).

Armed conflict has been an important part of the post-independence legacy of south Asia. Whether on the Afghan border with Pakistan, in Kashmir, in the Chittagong Hill Tracts, among Maoist rebels or in the north and east of Sri Lanka, armed conflict is a terrible reality that many women in south Asia have to face. Women are affected by armed conflict in different ways. First, they are often the victims of direct violence especially sexual violence by armed soldiers or militants. Rape during wartime is one of the oldest war crimes and is now clearly prohibited by the statute of the International Criminal Court (Articles 7,8). However none of the countries of south Asia have become parties to the ICC. There have been some prosecutions for custodial violence in south Asia. In Sri Lanka in the famous case of Krishanthy Kumaraswamy, the court handed the death penalty to the perpetrators. However, in most of the cases there is no prosecution and the perpetrators are unpunished [Special Rapporteur VAW 1994-2003]. Sexual violence during wartime continues in all parts of south Asia and there is a sense of impunity on the part of the perpetrators.

Another way in which women are affected during war time is as internally displaced persons (IDP). Eighty per cent of IDPs are women and children. As IDPs they live in terrible circumstances. They are given meagre rations, they live in large communal halls without any privacy often only separated by a sari. Women are often sexually harassed in these camps by officials and inmates and there are minimal sanitation facilities. They are also subject to restrictions on their freedom of movement. They often dream of returning home but are in these camps for a very long period of time. When the armed conflict is over, resettlement is an even longer process. They often find their lands and homes occupied or destroyed. They usually do not have the communal infrastructure to begin a new life and they are subject to a great deal of bureaucratic regulation. Women and children in these camps continue to have psychosocial problems and long-term adjustment problems. Women are also affected by war in that they become war widows, often losing their husbands. In very patriarchal societies that oppress and discriminate against women, these young widows have special problems and concerns. They become among the poorest and most vulnerable communities in the country [Tiruchandran 1999]. Research suggests that they survive because of the future they envision for their children.

In some wars women actually become combatants such as in Sri Lanka. Here the ambiguity of the Geneva Convention on the protection of women combatants raises a whole host of issues. Moreover, in the post-conflict situation, other parts of the world such as Colombia, point to obstacles in partriarchal societies. Women as warriors, though exciting because of the transgressing of gender roles, raise other issues relating to the realization women's rights within the framework of military imperatives and war.

Trafficking

Chamoli was 16 years old and living with her father and stepmother. Her step mother did not like her very much and used to beat her often. One day a young man came from outside to the village. Chamoli fell in love with him and he promised to marry her. She eloped with him to India. He then took her to a big house and he saw money exchange between her new lover and the madam of the house. After that her lover disappeared and she found she was in a brothel. She was literally tortured into submission. She had to service about ten customers a day and was living in a cubicle the size of a bed. Finally Maiti Nepal a Nepalese NGO came to her brothel and "rescued her". She then spent seven months in an Indian "protection home" before she was sent back to Nepal When she got there doctors as Maiti Nepal discovered that she was suffering from AIDS. Chamoli refuses to return to her family because of the shame and because of her fear of her step mother. (author's notes)

Trafficking of women and girls, especially into the big cities of India, remains a serious problem in the south Asian region. Increasingly young girls between the ages of 10 and 14 are trafficked to different parts of India from within India as well as Nepal and Bangladesh. In other countries there are smaller trafficked to enterprises taking place. It is estimated that about 2,00,000 young girls from Nepal in India of which 45,000 are in Mumbai alone. Women are often trafficked by close friends and family.

Sometimes trafficking is linked to traditional contexts and practices. In Nepal, the experience of the badi caste, who provided entertainment services to feudal elites and who now must respond to market forces has led to the trafficking of their daughters and wives who leave Nepal in search of a better future. Traditional temple dancers such as devadasis, jogins, matammas and deukis were once children pledged by their parents to the temple and who become sex workers associated with the temple. These women also become vulnerable to further trafficking once they become older.

Trafficking is also complicated by the legal regimes that are in place for the regulation of prostitution. Some countries in south Asia have "moralistic" legal regime that criminalise everything associated with prostitution—the sex worker, the client, the middlemen, etc. This is true especially in Islamic country of south Asia. Sri Lanka and India have the "abolitionist model" contained in the 1949 convention, where the women is seen as a victim and is not criminalised whereas those who exploit her prostitution are criminalised.

Though on the books, it is rarely implemented. In both these frameworks the criminal justice system is an integral part of the regime and abuse and corruption in the system often ends up victimises the trafficked women. This has led to many people in south Asia asking for more liberal legal regimes for prostitution to allow the sex worker a certain social legitimacy and more social and economic rights.

However, trafficking is perhaps most complicated by its link to migration. Research clearly shows that most of women who are trafficked have strong desire to migrate and are thereby abused in the process. Women desire to migrate often because there is abuse in the home, in the community or because of dire poverty. To counter trafficking by preventing women's migration is to lock them into domestic systems of oppression. Measures taken to prevent women from migrating such requiring permission of male member of the family or government sanction may actually compound the problem. What is needed is an effective system that prevents women from being abused during the process of migration this can only take place if the approach to trafficking is designed within a human rights framework.

The human rights framework would also require a different approach to the women survivor once she leaves sex work. Instead of the usual approach of "rescue", "rehabilitation" and "repatriation" which has conditioned the mainstream approach to trafficking, there is now an emphasis on consulting the women on what she really wants to do. Does she want to remain in sex work? Does she wish to return home? Does she wish to stay in her host country? Does she wish to go back to her parents? These approaches then require a partnership between the police, immigration officials and women's support groups who can counsel the women survivor. These approaches are not present in south Asia where the approach to trafficking is very much oriented towards rescue, rehabilitation (or protection) and repatriation.

Asha Rani was a young bride. Her poor family gave her a small dowry but after marriage her in-laws wanted another Rs. 5,000 or an auto-rickshaw. Her father who had seven daughters could not provide the amount. When he refused, the in-laws beat his daughter in front of his eyes. A few weeks later Asha Rani was dead, "burnt while making tea". According to her in-laws, her synthetic sari caught fire on the stove. But the post-mortem revealed otherwise. The Supreme Count finally ruled that she did not die of accident nor did she commit suicide. She was murdered [Umar 1998].

Domestic Violence

Newspaper pages in south Asia are full of tales of domestic violence. In 2002, 450 honour killings were reported in Pakistan, 15,000 young brides are burnt to death every year in India, and 10 women a week are subject to acid attacks in Bangladesh [OXFAM 2004]. Violence by intimate family members is one of south Asia's darkest legacies. Fourty per cent of all sexual abuse cases in India are about incest. In a survey on violence against women in India, 94 [per cent of the cases involved an offender who was a member of the family [Naved 2004].

The violence against women in south Asia often begins before birth. It is estimated the 50 million women are missing in India either through sex selective abortions, female infanticide or female neglect. So much so that the sex ratio in certain states of India is very disturbing. There are 79.3 girls for every 100 males in the Punjab and 87.8 girls for every 100 males in Gujarat [OXFAM 2004:10].

Domestic violence rates in south Asia does vary from community to community and depends on the questions on the questions asked. A survey of 1,842 women in Uttar Pradesh and Tamil Nadu in India presented a rate of 40 per cent of women interviewed stating they were victims of wife beating. In Pakistan, a survey of 1,000 women indicated that 55 per cent in the urban areas and 35 per cent in the rural areas stated that they were victims of domestic violence. In Sri Lanka, one survey put the figure at 60 per cent, another at 32 per cent [UNIFEM 2004:10].

Research on indicators for domestic violence in the region highlights issues such as the fact that children who, themselves are abused or who has witnessed violence in the family are far more likely to beat their wives than other children. In south Asia alcohol and drug use also accentuates domestic violence. Patriarchal societies where men control all decisions often witness greater violence when women seem to question or go outside the framework of such decisions. If a society seeks to resolve conflict through the use of violence then violence in the home is also on the increase. The lack of economic independence on the part of women and their inability to move out of a violent situation and state inaction against perpetrators of violence helps perpetuate a ideological belief that violence may even be justified and even if it is not, it is not a terrible matter that requires concerted action.

The insensitivity of the criminal justice system has also been highlighted in many studies. Police stations rarely respond though with the new police women desks this situation is marginally better. A survey of judges in the region (south Asia) pointed to the fact that 48 per cent of judges agreed that it was justifiable for men to beat their wives and 74 per cent endorsed the view that even in cases of violence the preservation of the family should be the primary concern.

The insensitivity of the criminal justice system has also been of action, ensure a trained and sensitive criminal justice system, support systems for victims, ensures sensitive health professionals and to also maintain data collection and analysis about the incidents of domestic violence. Some countries in south Asia, for example, India and Sri Lanka, have begun to respond to these standards in a progressive manner.

Rape and Sexual Harassment

Mathura was a young girl from the dalit community. She ran away from home and married her boyfriend. Her family threatened her and her husband. When she went to the police station to make a complaint, she was gang raped by the policemen. Her case so scandalized India, that Parliament passed an amendment to the penal code making special provisions to protect the rights of victims who are subject to rape in state custodial institutions.

Rape and sexual harassment continue to be

important issues in the south Asian context. In 1998, the Human Rights Commission of Pakistan. In India for the same year, there were over 15,000 reported cases while so many go unreported. Such cases are often compounded in the rural areas of gang rape of dalit women by upper caste men as an act of political violence. A CNN survey in New Delhi pointed to the fact that 50 per cent of all working women claimed that they were sexually harassed in the workplace. In Pakistan, the Alliance Against Sexual Harassment in the workplace claimed that 93 per cent of women working in the public and private sectors had experienced some form of harassment in the workplace. Marital rape and sexual violence as a means of initiation are also reported in some of these surveys, a factor that will influence the marriage relationship for years to come [UNIFEM 2004: 17]. This is the case even though marital rape is not a crime in all the countries of south Asia.

The issues of rape was what first galvanized the women's movement in India and to some extent in the other south Asian countries. The rape of the dalit girl Madura in a custodial setting led to a national campaign for the reform of the rape laws. The Law Commission set up to look into this matter decided that in cases of custodial rape the onus of proving consent would shift to the accused. In Sri Lanka penal reforms of 1995 gave more serious punishment for custodial violence but like its Indian counterpart called for mandatory enhanced punishments.

Feminists have been challenging the rape laws of their countries for over a generation now. The need to take away language like "against her will" that requires physical bruises, the need to make sure that a woman's past history is not introduced into the evidence and the need to get rid of evidentiary procedure that requires corroboration. The National Commission for Women in India draft amendment to the Indian Penal Code on issues relating to rape is very much along these lines.

In this context, given the terrible nature of the crimes against women many young legal scholars are questioning whether the legal systems can be effective in dealing with crimes against women and whether other alternatives to prosecution and punishment should be explored. Statistics for a given period in Mumbai show that of the 504 cases that were registered, only 469 were chargesheeted, of which there were 13 convictions, and 10 acquittals, the vast majority were pending trial or never really got to the trial stage [Agnes 1990:48]. Furthermore, feminists fear that the rape trial often becomes a "Pornographic spectacle" [Menon 200:91]. Even when judgments convict, the rape survivor emerges brutalized and sometimes a "scandal figure" in a still very patriarchal society. For this reasons most women continue to be silent when they are victims of sexual violence.

The inability of the legal systems to deliver justice in the case of women and the reliance on the prosecution arm of the state has created unease among some women's rights activists. They argue that reliance on the legal strategy alone is not enough and that a more broad based approach aimed at transforming attitudes and social structures is necessary [Kapoor and Cossman 1996].

Customary Practices

Samia was married to an abusive husband. One day she ran away from home stating that she wanted a divorce. There were rumours that she had found someone else. Finally her family said they were granting her wish. Her mother, her uncle and a strange came to the lawyer's chambers to discuss the case. Suddenly the stranger pulled a gun out and shot Samia and aimed over the head of the lawyer. The security in the office shot the stranger but mother and the uncle escaped taking one of the members of the law firm as hostage, who was later released. The police have not prosecuted the case since they felt it was an "honour" killing.

The failure of the law is particularly relevant when it comes to customary practices in a region that is violent toward women South Asia is perhaps the region with the largest number of customary practices that are violent toward women. The response to the international critique of such practices has been mixed. Some regard these as internal issues and not a concern to the rest of the world; some practices are justified by the internal logic of indigenous cultural system and any attempt to critique and eradicate such customs is part of the arrogant legacy of colonialism and westernisation. However, women's groups within these societies have also taken up these issues and highlighted them as evidence of the low status of women in south Asian societies. These customary practices are in conflict with the international obligations that south Asian states have voluntarily taken upon themselves. The charge of westernisation is also disingenuous since many of these societies are rapidly globalising and the question of culture seems primarily relevant only to the subordinate position of women. The duality between public and private has a special meaning in south Asia where scholars have claimed that the private is also seen as "eastern", "spiritual" and the domain of the women. To change customary practices would entail a necessary transformation of the private and therefore threaten the "eastern" and "spiritual" nature of south Asia societies [Chatterjee 1989]. As a result, attempts to eradicate customary practices that are violent toward women meet with local level resistance and require both a political as well as a legal approach.

Another customary practice that is associated with south Asia is the practice of bridge burning. Bride burning reached its height in the early 1990s. Dowry related murders increased from 437 deaths in 1983 to 4,856 in 1991 and to 5,582 in 1993; these are the reported cases [Umar 1998:12]. In Delhi, in the early 1980s, the frequency of unnatural deaths of housewives was one every 12 hours. While dowry in certain communities was linked to land and immovable property, giving women some sense of security, it has in the modern world become a morbid symptom of a customary practice. Today a dowry consists first, gifts to the bride in terms of clothes, jewellery and household gifts. Second dowry consists of luxury items for the husband, clothes, wristwatch, gold chain, etc; thirdly it may include immovable property written in the husband's name and finally modern electronic items such as television, fridges, video cassette players etc. [Umar 1998:67]. Material gifts and cash are paid to the bridegroom, who if he is widowed and then marries again receives dowry a second time.

Women are burned as brides either because of dowry, incompatibility between husband and wife, the rigidity of the divorce laws, or a desire to have son. In recent times the Indian penal code was amended to deal specifically with dowry deaths. Since 1986 the law has provided for punishment not less than seven years and up to life imprisonment for a husband or family member if a women's death occurs due to burns, injuries or other unnatural circumstances and she was subjected to cruelty or harassment in connection with dowry [Lawyers' Collective 1992]. The number of dowry deaths has decreased in recent years due to the penal sanctions but they do still occur in many parts of south Asia.

Acid attacks are often directed at women who reject the advances of men or by family members in the protection of honour. These attacks have received recent attention in Bangladesh but still continue in certain parts. Linked to the concept of honour it is difficult to eradicate as long as women's emotional and sexual behaviour are seen as reflecting on the honour of the men who are intimately connected to them.

Another south Asian practice that has received international attention is the practice of sati or window burning in certain parts of India. The case of Roop Kanwar, who in the late 1980s committed sati on her husband's pyre in a public spectacle created major national and international furore. Sati is often always committed under coercive circumstances and a tolerance of sati would make many families urge their young windows to commit sati to prevent having to take care of them. For this reason women's group are not only argued against sati as a practice but also the ideology of sati. Luckily the Indian state responded firmly [Hawley 1994].

The practice of sati reminds us that violence and discrimination against windows is a common cultural practice in south Asia. Besides sati, this often manifests itself in witch killings. In Bihar in average of 200 women are killed every year as witches. In any of these cases there is some dispute over land with the victim's husband's family. They lack of economic independence and security for a widow makes her particularly vulnerable. Supposed to be inauspicious, she is socially secluded and discriminated against. If her presence drains the family of its resources, in some cases there is a cultural form of killing or exclusion that allows families to deal with unwanted widows. Again the criminal justice system rarely prosecutes families for their windows.

Another customary practice in south Asia that denotes violence award women is the practice of child marriage. In Nepal 40 per cent of marriages involve girls under the age of 15 [UNIFEM 2004:16]. In Pakistan the "watta satta" marriage is another form of marriages that violates the rights of women. Women become part of barter between men. A woman is given in marriage to a man in return for another woman. The case of 12-year old Reshma, she was given in a watta satta marriage took place after a terrible dispute between the two families. On her wedding night her husband shot her dead claiming she had committed adultery [OXFAM 2004:8]. These traditional forms of marriage held together by the concept of honour and community deeply oppress women but are so firmly embedded in south Asia that unless there is concerted action with the state taking lead, such practices will never change.

At the root of much of the violence against women in customary practices is the palpable son preference seen in south Asian societies. Amartya Sen has chronicled how with regard to food, hospitals and schooling there is terrible discrimination against the girl child. Young girls are taken to hospital only if they are very ill, young girls are more malnourished than young boys and in schooling, only 15 per cent of girls in rural primary schools go beyond the fifth grade. They gender gap in school enrolment is 14 per cent in India, 19 per cent in Nepal and 24 per cent in Pakistan [UNIFEM 2004: 14-16]. This son preference and the discrimination against the girl child lasts a lifetime leading to a lifecycle of violence and discrimination.

Violence Against Women and Masculinity

Customary practices such as those outlined above require the state to create a normative framework that frowns on such practices and crimnalises those who engage in such activities. However, for the most part, because of political unpopularity, states shy away from insisting on international standards on the protection of women form violence. As a result, there is a sense that the violence is "normal", or "usual" and that severe action should not be taken against the perpetrators. This normalisation of violence shows the interlinkage between ideology and violence against women. In Bangladesh in a recent survey the majority or men argued that violence against their wives was all right in certain circumstances as corrective punishment

[UNIFEM 2004]. This normalisation prevents men from seeing the violence as wrong, prevents women from asserting that the violence is a violation and paralyses the criminal justice system in trying to attain justice.

Another linkage that is often made is that women's lack of economic independence and empowerment has a great deal to do with the levels of violence in south Asian societies. Women's lack of economic security forces them to put up with extreme acts of violence for the sake of survival. Inheritance laws and practices, the lack of access to land, the lack of education and the denial of mobility contribute keeping women locked into situations from which there is no escape. David Levinson in an 90-country study found that the lack of economic independence is one of the main reasons for violence against women [Levinson 1989].

In south Asia women's access to economic resources has always been limited. Bina Aggarwal and Govind Kelkar have written extensively about these issues with regard to India and south Asia. Since a large part of south Asia is agricultural, systems of inheritance laws and cultural practices preclude women from having access to important economic resources [Kelkar 1993:117]. Some south Asia societies following Islamic laws give differential access to inheritance between sons and daughters. Nevertheless, even in societies and personal law systems where there is equal inheritance, the right of the testator to will his property often results in women being excluded and in being restricted to "dowry" property. Dowry, a negative customary practice then becomes the marker of a woman's inheritance. As Gail Omvedt writes, "The basic economic dependence of women, their property lessness and resourcelessness renders them fearfully weak in standing up and challenging the violence and power that is used against them in society" [National Law School Journal 1993:120].

The right of windows to inherit and to live secure lives free from violence, social ostracism and discrimination still remains an important need in the south Asian context. Poorer women, who have no access to inheritance or land, are economically marginalised, earning 40 per cent of male wages, doing the more labour intensive tasks and often sexually abused and raped by the upper caste landlords on whose fields they work. The rape of dalit women by upper caste men in India remains a major area of human rights violations having casts, class and gender implications. In land rights movements, women fought for "izzat", the right to live in dignity and to be free from the threat of rape along with the right to parity in agricultural wages and access to land. The discrimination with regard to the distribution of land by the state is also manifold. Govind Kelkar in studying land distribution by the Bihar Kisan Saniti in 1989 points to how only five women (three of whom were widows) received land compared to 110 men who did and that of the 120 acres distributed women received only 7.85 acres. Discussions urging women to receive land was not well received by the male leaders of the village who saw any such suggestion as a major threat [Kelkar 1989:137].

Models of masculinity in the south Asian region also contribute to violence against women. In certain communities, violence is closely linked to honour and the assertion of masculine status. If being a man means controlling and domesticating your wife, then behaviour patterns emerge accordingly. Given the deeply held values and time honoured "masculine" traditions, changing these models and expectations may only take place over generations. For this, there have to be other masculine non-violent traditions that capture the imagination of young men. In modern times, some of these traditions are merging in south Asia but they are in a nascent phase [Chopra 2004].

Pradeep Jeganathan in a study on masculinity in Sri Lanka points to two models of masculinity that appear to exist side by side. The first, based on traditional notions of restraint, point to a respectable, responsible adult male who protects traditional virtues. This is perhaps the model inherited from the nationalist phase and Sinhalese preoccupation with shame and fear of ridicule. The other model centres around model notions of "fearlessness" whether it is the soldier, the politician, the guerrilla, the "criminal thug" and this fearlessness contains elements of criminality and violence. The emergence of this masculine category in post independent south Asia as a dominant paradigm has worrisome implications for violence against women [Jeganathan 2000].

Thomas Michael Walle's study into Pakistani models of masculinity also point to this dichotomy between what he calls the "moral" model—i.e., those men who follow the edicts of the Koran and the "immoral" model of the drinker and the womaniser. Both exist side by side and are deployed accordingly. In both models women are seriously compromised as the "moral" man carries with him a legacy of patriarchy and the "immoral" man a hint of violence, wantonness and eventual abandonment. According to Walle "loved-marriages" are discredited in this society and is an implication of weakness—a man who takes his woman too seriously [Walle 2004].

Radhika Chopra in her work points to a variety of masculinity models in India—the householder who is the great provider, the Gandhian renouncer. The nationalist depiction of Gandhian "effeminate" males in India has been replaced with notions of a virulent Hindu male confronting "the other", especially "the Muslim". This "restoration" of an aggressive Hindu masculinity also has implications for violence against women. Ashis Nandy's famous article (1998) pointing to the "feminine" vision of Gandhi and the so–called masculine vision of his assassin seems to have played itself out in post-independent India with aggressive, violent manifestations of masculinity taking the upper hand in the 1990s.

Linked to notions of masculinity is also belief in the proper emotional and sexual behaviour of women. A great part of violence against women has to deal with female sexuality. Rape is about sexual violence, trafficking is often about sex work, sexual harassment is about a woman's refusal to have sex with her husband and many so-called customary practices such as honour killings or female genital mutilation are linked to the control of female sexuality. For this reasons it is important that the protection of women from violence must be accompanied by the recognition of the reproductive rights and freedoms of women. This linkage is extremely important if we are to create conditions for women to be free from the fear of violence.

Costs of Violence Against Women

Violence against women has costs for the individual victims as well for the society at large. With regard to individual victims, the first cost is that of damage to the health of women. The WHO report (2002) lists the costs of domestic violence abuse on women in terms of health consequences. These include physical consequences, such as injuries, bruises, welts, disability, chronic paint, syndrome, fractures, gastrointestinal disorders, lacerations and abrasions, ocular damage and reduced physical functioning. It has sexual and reproductive consequences such as gynaecological disorders, infertility, pelvic inflammatory disease, miscarriage and pregnancy complications, sexual dysfunction, sexually transmitted disease, unsafe abortion and unwanted pregnancy. It has psychological and behavioural consequences which include alcohol and drug abuse, depression and anxiety, eating and sleeping disorders, feelings of shame and guilt, phobias and panic disorders, physical inactivity, poor self-esteem, post-traumatic stress disorder, psychosomatic disorders, smoking, suicidal behaviour, and unsafe sexual behaviour. The health consequences can also be fatal such as homicide, suicide, maternal mortality and AIDS-related mortality. As a result of all these complications abused women are also long-term users of a country's health services and facilities with the hospital as an important location for women victims of violence.

Violence against women also exacts economic costs for the women concerned and therefore for the society. Research shows that women with a history of partner violence were more likely to be unemployed, to experience job turnover, and a negative impact job performance [UNIFEM 2004:29]. In Canada a study states that violence against women costs Canada 1.6 billons dollars a year in terms of medical care and loss of productivity [UNIFEM 2004:31].

Violence against women also has a profound effect on the children in the family. There appears to be a correlation between violence against women and child mortality. Children who witness violence are at a higher risk for a whole range of emotional and behavioural problems including anxiety, depression, poor school performance and low self-esteem. The children are also more likely to become abusers when they become adults. A study in often, children aged 6-36 months had a higher risk of stunted and wasted growth than did children in communities where beatings were not reported [UNIFEM 2004:31].

Perhaps the greatest consequence of violence against women is fear and the chilling effect it has on women's empowerment and mobility. A recent study in Bangladesh points to the fact that only about 18 per cent of women feel comfortable enough to leave their houses alone. Less than 1 per cent of working women said they felt safe in the workplace, citing dark corridors and ill lit places as sites they fear; 81 per cent of women stated that they would not go out unless they covered themselves properly for fear of violence [UNIFEM 2004:19-24]. Fear and insecurity then condition women's lives in a profound way because of anticipated violence. There is fear of the violence and fear of the shame if violence was to occur. Living in anticipation of violence curtails their priorities and the choices they make for the future. It makes women search out men for protection rather than companionship and makes women dependent and vulnerable. Fear then socialises women to conform to the very ideological norms that ensure their subordination.

State and Civil Society

Responses in South Asia

International instruments such as CEDAW recommendation 19 and the UN declaration on violence against women spell out the measures that states should take to eradicate violence against women in their societies. The so-called "responsibilities" of due diligence duty as spelled out in international instruments involve:

(i) The duty of pass legislation and other measures that provide a frame work for preventing and punishing crimes of violence against women;

(ii) The duty to enact effective procedures and to train and sensitise the criminal justice system to ensure that they take violence against women to be a serious issue that demands concerted action. Included in the criminal justice process are the police, prosecutors, judiciary and forensic medical professionals;

(iii) The duty to provide support services for victims of violence such as shelters, legal and psychological counselling, training in income generating endeavours, etc, with the assistance of NGOs and other civil society organisations;

(iv) The duty to collect data and conduct research

into what is often an invisible phenomenon so as to identify the problems related to violence against women in any given society; and

(*v*) The duty to comply with international obligations and the duty to report or international treaty bodies.

All the governments of the SAARC region have responded positively to the challenges posed by violence against women in their region. In the last decade, there has been a great deal of advances, especially in the area of standard setting and the enactment of policies and programmes. Though a great deal may not have changed at the local level, the policy framework has been developed in most of the countries of the region.

Bangladesh has responded to the challenges posed by violence against women in the region by declaring openly in its national strategy for economic growth, poverty reduction and social development that it plans to substantially reduce or eliminate violence against women and children by 2015. In 2000, Bangladesh adopted the Prevention of Oppression against Women and Children Act which deals comprehensively with crimes of violence against women. Bangladesh has also set up a National Advisory Council for the prevention for violence against women with committees to prevent VAW in every district. There are also four investigative cells in the police station and a multisectoral programme which was adopted in 2000 that tries to combine the efforts of the health services, the police, access to justice and public awareness.

India too has taken positive measures with regard

to violence against women. With regard to sex selective abortions, in 1994, India adopted the Pre-Conception and Pre-Natal Diagnostic Techniques Act and this has been amended twice as recently as 2003. The recently tabled domestic violence legislation is quite NGOs especially the Lawyers Collective. In contains many provisions combining civil and criminal remedies and providing support for women survivors of violence. India is also in the process of adopting other legislation with relevance for fighting violence against women.

The Indian government is also considering the possibility of introducing legislation on trafficking. At the moment the main legislation to tackle the problem of trafficking is Immoral Traffic (Prevention) Act. Thought the act does not criminalise sex work, maintaining brothel, etc.

In Nepal in the last decade, a great deal has been done in the area of trafficking. The ministry of women, children and social welfare has proposed a new bill to replace the Traffic in Human Beings (Control) Act. The bill broadens the definition of trafficking and has strong provisions with regard to punishment and evidentiary procedure. In the late 1990s, the ministry also adopted a national anti-trafficking policy and a rehabilitation home for victims of trafficking. The Human Rights Commission of Nepal also created a National Rapporteur on Trafficking.

In Pakistan, though many crimes of violence against women are dealt with under the Offence of Zina (Enforcement of Hudood) Ordinance, which has difficult evidentiary provisions with regard to the women victim, the National Commission on the Status of Women has now been requested to review all laws, rules and regulations affecting the status of women. The Commission also set up a committee of experts to review the Hudood and Zina Ordinances. In 2004, the Parliament in Pakistan adopted legislation criminalizing honour killings with strong punishments for the perpetrators. The law treats honour killings as an aggravated form of murder. The Pakistan Supreme Court has also stated that honour killings are murder and violate a woman's fundamental right. Crisis centres have been established for women in distress in Islamabad, Vehari, Lahore and Sahiwal.

In Sri Lanka, the decade witnessed the drafting of the Penal Code Amendments in 1995 which was a major step forward with regard to meeting the challenge of violence against women. Rape is defined without the limiting words "against her will" and special provisions exist for judicially separated couples and statutory rape. There is enhanced punishment for custodial rape, rape of a pregnant woman, rape of someone under 18, rape of a mentally disabled person and gang rape. There are also provisions for mandatory sentencing. In Sri Lanka a draft law on domestic violence is also pending. The draft law defines domestic violence broadly and provides for a broad range of remedies including interim and permanent protection orders, emergency monetary relief and compensation.

The countries of south Asia have all ratified CEDAW though some of them have done so with reservations. The countries of south Asia have also signed the SAARC Convention on Preventing and Combating the Trafficking in Women and Children for prostitution. The Trafficking Convention defines trafficking narrowly and it is not in conformity with the international definition. It provides for cooperation among member states, repatriation and rehabilitation of women survivors, and has certain measures to ensure prevention [Report on Violence against Women E/CN. 4/2003/75/Add.1].

Conclusion

The above survey points to the fact that all the states in the south Asian region have responded to some of the challenges posed by violence against women in the region. Many have passed laws or are entertaining draft laws to deal with some of the important questions. Ten years after Beijing, it is still a concern that except for India none of the countries of the region have adopted domestic violence legislation or made the necessary changes to anti-trafficking legislation. However programmes and policies are in place and a great deal of activity has been conducted by ministries dealing with women and welfare, national commissions and individual government department. There have been many training programmes also for senior level policy officers and other members of the criminal justice system.

The changes in south Asia have also been made possible by the activism of civil society and the foresight of many NGOs. They have conducted research, suggested legal reform and put in place constructive programmes that actually assist women victims of violence. They have trained policemen, lobbied politicians and judges and also put together shelters and crisis centres. They have taken cases to court, demonstrated for women's rights and in some countries mobilized people at the risk to their own lives. They have counseled and cared for many victims of violence breaking their silence and allowing them to regain their dignity.

Research from around the world points to the fact that violence against women can only be combated if there is a healthy partnership between women's groups and the state apparatus. While women's groups must protect their independence, on certain issues they have to work effectively with the criminal justice system, joining forces to protect the rights of women victims. However, this also poses a major dilemma. The decade ends with the triumph of a certain "law and order feminism" which aims at punishing the perpetrator, using draconian provisions in the law. Whether in trafficking, rape or sexual harassment, there is a punishment rhetoric that belies a complex reality. South Asia is particularly receptive to this excess of law enforcement. Provisions in trafficking legislation, in sexual offences legislation, in preventing women form migrating procedures, are so draconian that they raise questions about the human rights of the perpetrators and an over reliance on the criminal justice system to solve complex social questions. Thought they provide an immediate sense of something being done, in the long run they pose serious dilemmas. In the end judges and juries just do not convict if they feel that the law is too harsh or unreasonable. Fighting violence against women will only succeed if it is done through the lens of human rights, protecting the rights and dignity of the women survivor while ensuring a fair trial for the perpetrator. Any other course of action will not stand the test of time and important legislation will fall into disuse.

Fairness must be a central concern for women even when they are dealing with abusers. Moreover, the law is an important tool but it is one of the many strategies available to women. While fighting for justice through the legal system, there should also be attempts to put in place education policies, health strategies and community level programmes that promote equality between men and women and teach non-violent methods of resolving conflict. A multipronged approach to violence against women will result in far-reaching changes, transforming attitudes and practices so that women and men can live in equality and dignity.

5

Women in Governance at Global Level

South Asia presents us with a paradox. It has more powerful women politicians than any other set of countries in the world. Women have been prime ministers, leaders of major parties, heads of state and regional governments. Chandrika Kumaratunga in Sri Lanka, Sonia Gandhi in India, Benazir Bhutto in Pakistan and Khaleda Zia in Bangladesh are the most famous examples. Yet, overall women's political participation is dismal. The membership of women in the Parliaments of these countries has ranged between 6 and 8 per cent during the last few decades; the predominance of women political leaders at the highest level seems to have no implication for even the slightly lower level of the elites who normally send members to Parliament. And, at the lowest level, village politics have been in the hands of men, with women confined to domestic duties. Even in the areas of greatest community concern to women, for instance, water and forest management, they have little say.

The countries of south Asia have taken steps to

remedy this situation. The main method chosen is that of reservation (quotas in electoral bodies). India and Bangladesh since 1993, and Pakistan since 2000 all reserve 33 per cent of the seats in local village governmental institutions for women. At the national level in India, a bill for reserving one-third seats for women in Parliament has been pending for several years; all major parties have expressed commitment to it and it continues to be debated fiercely though it has not yet been passed. In addition, at the level of community management, programmes in almost countries for management of natural resources have included or featured women (such as the "joint forest management" or JFM Programmes). Yet, all these have clearly been insufficient, and the method of quotas to increase women's political participation is still opposed by many.

Obstacles to Participation

The obstacles to women's equal participation in governance are deeply embedded in south Asian social and cultural patterns. The patriarchal nature of most of these countries is starkly shown by Amartya Sen's criteria of "missing women". Most south Asian countries have a low sex ratio, i.e., the ratio of women to men. What Sen did was to calculate the number of women who would be alive today if such countries had "normal" ratios (equivalent to those of Europe and North America, or south-east Asian countries). This method gives us a figure that can be said to represent one crucial measure of the meaning of "patriarchy" for women. For India, the number was approximately to 40 million, a major proportion of the estimated 100 million that Sen calculated was the cost of anti-women discrimination for the world as a whole. Sri Lanka, with more equalitarian kinship patterns, is an exception to this. A later analysis by Dreze and Sen calculated the incidence of missing women at 35-37 million in India for 1986) and found most differences occurred after the age of one [Dreze and Sen 1995: 141-44]. This is a result of maltreatment, less access to medical care, less food and a general arduous and toiling existence.

In the case to India this extreme form of patriarchy is linked to the caste system: the maintenance of caste boundaries through bans on intermarriage ("roti-beti vyavahar") requires a high degree of control over sexuality; and, generally, over the independence of women. Caste is identified with brahminic Hinduism, but some form of caste also exists in the "Muslim" countries of Bangladesh and Pakistan and in "Buddhist" Sri Lanka, though historically it has been much less severe among non-Hindus, lacking both Brahmins at the top and untouchables at the bottom. Kinship structures in most of south Asia are still patrilineal and patrilocal: inheritance is solely through the male line, and after marriage the girl goes off to live with her husband's family. In north India and much of Pakistan, this often also means out of the village of her birth. She may continue to visit her natal family (especially for her first childbirth), but after marriage she essentially is taken as a member of her husband's family. This means that parents cannot realistically expect much from daughters except as a burden, especially with dowries. It is sons, not daughters, who will care for them when they are old. "Daughters are not ours, they belong to other people", an old saying in western India, refers to the implications of these kinship structures, which are deeply embedded and hard to change.

In rural and poor families, daughters-in-law are main workers of the household; they cook, clean, care for children and for old people. There is still little mechanisation to to help them with these burdens, though refrigerators, washing machines, TV are making a big entry into rural areas. Even TVs can be called "labour saving" in that they relieve housework's drudgery! However, a "women's place in the home" still defines women's positions. Public space and work outside the home are secondary; even employed women turn over the earnings to their husbands.

Girls are socialized to be mothers, wives and workers under others' authority. Their home responsibilities are endless; even when young, they usually help in the home and care for younger siblings, and middle class people using maid servants find that the woman usually brings her daughter along to help. Yet, in spite of this year and ongoing labour, women are always depicted as weaker than men, which in turn, justify "protectiveness" and reluctance to let women go out of the house. In almost all countries, the difference between men and women is marked by laterally fostered strong differences in dress and behavioural patterns. Customs of "purdah" exist not only among Muslims, but also among Hindus in rural India, where women in more "respectable caste" traditional families are expected to cover their faces before men, and sari ends are worn over the head, sometimes blocking the face. Women avoid the presence of non-kin males. Religious fundamentalism increases this purdah behaviour and efforts to keep women out of public life. Women following new, "revealing" fashions have been attacked by fundamentalists of all kinds. Overall, religious fundamentalism is inimical to women taking part in politics.

However, this issue of fundamentalism and religion has to be qualified by noting that women assert themselves within these movements too, and at the larger political level, the more "religious" parties of south Asia also have some prominent women; for instance, the prime minister of Bangladesh belongs to the more Muslim-identified of the two manor political parties, while in India the Hindu-nationalist Bharatiya Janata Party has two women among its chief ministers. The supremely secured Communist parties, in contrast, have no high level political women, with the exception of a recent induction of one woman into the politburo of the Communist Party of India (Marxist).

A final obstacle to women's political participation is the intensely competitive nature of politics itself. In the countries of south Asia, politics is a lucrative source of income and power which men attempt control. Data for India suggest that the reluctance of political parties to put up women candidates is a crucial factor in barring women from a role in governance. A study of the 2004 parliamentary elections by Rajeshwari Deshpande shows that a major factor in women's low winning percentage was at the interested was 12.4 per cent—compared to 9.8 per cent for men Deshpande 2004: 5433].

Community Management

Turning to specific areas of governance, we might hope to see the greatest possibilities of women's empowerment in the management of community resources (land, water and forests) simply because this is a local matter, where promotion of community control could allow women's participation without requiring them to move far from their homes. Further, where natural resources assume the most importance, it is for communities that are "tribal" (indigenous) or often poor and these communities have the greatest traditional work participation and relative independence of women. But in reality, women have little power here also.

Of natural resources, it is in the forest areas that communities have traditionally had control and that many current campaigns and programmes exist for increasing this control. In India, joint forest management (JFM) has been a programme running for some time—for over 30 years in the state of West Bengal where it was first initiated, and almost as long in some other areas. With communities getting responsibility, however, women have not necessarily benefited.

Why not? A major problem has been that the "joint" aspect of JFM does not really empower the communities. The programme generally includes a contract between a village community and the state; the villagers provide protection of degenerated forest areas, and in return receive a good share (usually a half) of the revenue from the timber once sold. While the forest area is growing, there is some provision of access to non-timber forest produce (NTFP), though this never includes the more lucrative products such as cashew nuts. However, this does not really mean community control; often the villagers do not even sell the timber themselves but receive only a share of the revenue and the marketing remains in the hands of the forest department.

Further, the structure of the programme creates a division of interest in the villages. Some communities are more dependent than others on access to non-timber forest produce; and these are usually the poorer castes and adivasi communities. As Madhu Sarin has shown, the result of most JFM programmes has been to decrease the access to NTFP, further, women were not initially conceived as major participants; rather participation has been through households, and the result of JFM has been increase income going to male heads of householders, who are by definition the shares in timber revenue, and discriminate against the poor. For example, a study of JFM over 30 years in West Bengal in a sal-coppice forest showed that net worth of employment generated by forest department increased from 0 to Rs. 4,67,000, but the loss of income suffered by 30 per cent of households selling firewood as head loaders declined from Rs. 13,65,000 to 0 during period [Sarin 1997: 309]. This has affected the women in poor families the most. Women, who the most active gatherers of NTFP have often been deprived of access. Further, women from the families of the dominant groups, who will benefit from the final sale of timber, have been mobilised against the women of poorer gathering communities.

Some reforms have been made in JFM programmes, both in West Bengal and in subsequent programmes in other states. In 1991, West Bengal legislated "joint membership" for women and men of households in JFM and some states provided for one woman and one man representative for each household. This is a small step forward. Nevertheless it is clear that the introduction of some community share does not necessarily have favourable implications for women's empowerment. Where women remain excluded from property ownership—and this is true not only among higher caste communities, but also among the poorer and indigenous groups—they will be excluded from any real control of the process of forest management.

Even where local control has some meaning, interaction with the state bureaucracy has adverse implications for women. The Indian Forest Service excluded women until 1979. By 1995 there were only 72 women Indian Forest Service officers out of 2,576—less than 3 per cent [Ibid:312]. Women often face lack of cooperation—and particularly the head load workers and gatherers of NTFP who come into direct conflict with them.

An imaginative programme of lease holding of forests by the poor in Nepal has shown that some of these obstacles can be overcome. The Nepal Forest Act of 1993 provides for the possibility of leasehold forestry, in which forests are handed over to any corporate body. This has meant, in many areas, leasing blocks of degraded forest lands to groups of poor households and giving then training in management. The result has been improved vegetative cover of the leased land, and increased income for the families, from fodder production and the manure provided for terrace agriculture. With a high outmigration of men from the area, the project introduced a focus on women, and women only groups for leasehold forestry were formed. Training was geared to women, and they were provided credit. The result was a greater participation of women in public activities, increased self-confidence, a reduction of labour time in collecting fuel and fodder and other benefits for women [Nathan and Shreshta 2004: 248-54].

In water management, specific attempts have been made to give a role to women. Water is a crucial resource for women, and women are the primary fillers of water, who in times of drought have to wander miles to bring water for household needs. Both India and Pakistan have had special governmental and NGO programmes focusing on women's irrigation management. Class and caste differences among women are also being recognized. One important example has been Self-Employed Women's Organisation (SEWA) in India. In Gujarat, SEWA launched a regional development programme to provide water and sanitation in Banaskantha district in 1988. Over a 10-year period women have played a critical role in village water committees, deciding priorities for distribution, looking after maintenance of community water resources, and managing funds mobilised by the villages. SEWA also provides "water loans" to women to finance access to water resources.

At the end of the 1990s, after severe drought conditions, SEWA organised a "Women, Water and Work Campaign" to mobilise women in nine districts to win a voice in water management. As Reema Nanavaty, a leader of SEWA, points out, "political as it may appear, we need to build collective organised strength of women as water users, managers, as owners. Without membership-based, democratic and active alliances of women water-users, the women will remain isolated" [Nanavaty 2000].

This has had only partial results, as shown by Sarah Ahmed's study of two villages where women have fought for access. In Kharati in Kheda district, a women of tailor caste, Meenaben, led a campaign that successfully got first a tanker and then a pipeline from a sweet water source provide drinking water for the village. However, among her opponents was the woman sarpanch, from the dominant thakur caste, and the village panchayat now successfully claims the achievement and has succeeded in isolating Meenaben [Ahmed 2000: 14-16]. The Gujarat example thus also shows that where women are excluded from general political institutions, they are not likely to have much power in community management of resources. Fighting for women's role in management of requires a simultaneous all-around fight for local poiitical power and, at the cultural level, for community recognition women's capacities.

Local Governance

The "village square" has been a male area in south Asia, reserved by custom for men. Traditional "panchayats" or governing bodies worked as caste communities, and were dominated by men of the village elite. Women were simply not members, though their issues were often taken up. However, within the independence movement, Gandhian political traditions valorized the traditional village institutions (though dalits, organised under Ambedkar, despised them), and when independence came, India named its local self-government institutions as "panchayati raj". The idea was to transform the community itself through the experience of self-government; what was emphasised in the hope from panchayats was empowerment of the people at the local level, while the repressive features of traditional Indian panchayat governments were rather conveniently ignored.

Quite expectedly, for a long time, whatever local self-government existed had little effect on gender relations. In India, a handful of women, usually one in each village, were nominated as members of the panchayat. Yet, their participation remained nominal; most did not even bother to attend the meetings but simply gave their "thumbprint" as signature to whatever decisions were taken.

This began to change in the late 1970s and early 1980s with the rise of a newly vigorous women's movement. The report the committee on the Status of Women, issued as Towards Equality in 1974, discussed the issue of political power and recommended women's quotas at the panchayat level. Women's aspirations began to rise as well. There were isolated examples of women attempting to enter the panchayats. Over a decade these challenges began to grow. For example, women in Indoli (a small village in satara district of western India) put up an "all-women" panel for local elections in 1985. They lost, rather overwhelmingly, with the political bosses of the villages challenging husbands of the candidates, "why don't you put on bangles?".

Then in 1986, the Shetkari Sanghatana, then at its height as an independent farmers' organisation, held a massive women's conference. The organisation, claimed to remain "non-political" though activists were always pressured to take part in elections. Men would sponsor women for public office, but not stand themselves. The conference gave a call to all political parties, in particular, Left and dalit (low-caste)-based parties to take part in the campaign to form all-women panels. All parties hedged, arguing that "we cannot find so many women". There was also an internal resistance within the Sanghatana itself, but this was overcome and women began to come forward enthusiastically [Omvedt 1990].

Though district elections were postponed, more and more women gained some awareness of their rights, and asserted themselves vigorously in local (village) elections. By the early 1990s, some 10-11 all women panels had been elected in various villages throughout the state. Most of these were in areas of the Shetkari Sanghatana, but some were outside of it. Women reported facing great obstacles, but at the same time achieving sense of self-respect and empowerment [Gala 1990, 1997]. All women panchayats began to be reported here and there in other states also, for example, West Bengal.

This was the background to the 73rd Constitutional Amendment Act in 1993. Rajiv Gandhi, then prime minister, had earlier identified himself with aspirations for local control in panchayati raj, and in the process of restructuring local panchayats, the act mandated a one-third representation to women at the village, taluka, and districts level as well as in urban municipalities. The result was bring over a million women into direct political participation. (It also had the effect of stopping the movement for all-women panchayat bodies, since it was easy for the Shetkari Sanghatana to accept the reserved seats.) But the process of giving women a more fair representation in local governmental bodies had begun.

Bangladesh also has quotas for women in local self-government institutions. Such representation was stipulated in the fundamental principle of this Constitution adopted after independence. Then, in 1993 as in India, an act of Parliament provided for direct election of reserved seats for women in the local councils, and the first elections under this were held in the 1997 [Global Database 2004], bringing about 12,000 women into local bodies.

In Pakistan, the Devolution of Power Plan (a local government plan) was adopted in March 2000, reserving 33 per cent seats and district level. In local councils, with an increase in the number of councils, about 70,000 women are now gaining experience self-government (Report on Local Self-Government: Pakistan 2000]. However, members of the tehsil and district councils are directly elected by the elected councilors at the local level.

In contrast, in Sri Lanka, several political proposals for quotas for women were made between 1998 and 2000 but were abandoned. In 2002, calls for quotas were renewed. The minister of women's affairs declared that the People's Alliance government would draft legislation to provide a minimum of 25 per cent representation of women in all elected bodies from the national parliamentary level to village councils. But this was not done, and in contrast to its better record on overall human development and gender development measures, Sri Lanka has the lowest level of participation of women in local governance. Women were 4 per cent of provincial councils, 2.3 per cent of municipal councils, and 1.4 per cent of urban councils as of June 2000 [CAPWIP 2001].

In Nepal, 20 per cent of seats are reserved in local government institutions for women by the Local Self Government Act of 1999. This includes municipalities and wars (in villages) and has resulted in catapulting about 40,000 women into political activities.

Local Governance Reservations

Reservations in local self-government institutions for women have been in operation for a little more than a decade. Training programmes have been organised by NGOs and sometimes sponsored by the government; in many cases they have worked to bring together elected panchayat women members and provides training in the issues of local government as well as some minimum feminist ideology. Even conservative organisations, for instance, Jamaat-i-Islami in Pakistan, often have such training programmes; the very existence of the quotas puts some pressure on political parties not simply to bring in women, but also to ensure that they can be effective as party representatives.

Initially, women elected under the new quotas found themselves at a disadvantage not only because of traditional cultural and social barriers, but also due to simple lack of experience and resentment among the various male political leaders that the participation of women was forced on them. (The contrast here with those rare villages in which they willingly elected all-women or women-dominated panchayats would be useful to investigate in more depth.)

A few academic studies are now available. Evelyn Hust studied in women two villages in different areas of Orissa, a coastal region and an inland region once part of a princely state. She found that while there were no dramatic changes, women did make some gains, most notably that of increasing their mobility and right to mix with other people, an enhanced status, and increased self-confidence[Hust 2004; 262-65]. Women continued to be less knowledgeable than men about the nature and issues of local political corruption was much affected by their presence or that there were different developmental preferences. Hust sees the most important aspects of empowerment in the symbolic recognitions of women's political role and in fact, that women in general had a new access to their elected representatives. Finally, there was a significant regional difference: in the coastal village, with its greater history of nationalist movement participation, women gained more in terms of autonomy (Ibid: 265).

A study by Damayanti Sridharan and Veena Kodic [cited in Jain 2005] of the all-India situation shows that only about 35 per cent of the women they studied came from political families; while this seems large, the fact that 65 per cent came from families with no other political representatives shows that the many women indeed could act on their own.

REFERENCES

Agarwal, Bina (1994): *A Field of One's Own: Gender and Land Rights in South Asia*, Cambridge University Press, Cambridge.

Appadurai, Arjun (2004): 'The Capacity to Aspire: Culture and the terms of Recognition' in Vijayendra Rao and Micheal Walton (eds), *Culture and Public Action*, Stanford University Press, Stanford.

Bourdieu, Pierre (2001): *Masculine Domination*, Stanford University Press, Stanford.

Deolaliker, Anil B (2005): *Attaining the Millennium Development Goals in India*, Oxford University Press and the World Bank.

Dreze, Jean and Amartya Sen (2002): *India Development and Participation*, Oxford University Press, Delhi.

Douglas, Mary (2004): 'Traditional Culture – Let's Hear No More about It' in Vijayendra Rao and Micheal Walton (eds), *Culture and Public Action*, Stanford University Press, Stanford.

Elson, Diane (1991): *Male Bias and Development Process*, Manchester University Press, Manchester.

Government of Bangladesh (2002): Statistical Profile of Women in Bangladesh, Ministry of Women and Children Affairs, Bangladesh Bureau of Statistics and Ministry of Planning, Dhaka.

Government of the People's Republic of Bangladesh (2003): Bangladesh - A National Strategy for Economic Growth, Poverty Reduction and Social Development, March.

Government of India (1991-2001): *Census of India*, Office of Registrar General and Census Commissioner.

Government of India and Academic Foundation (2004): *State of the Indian Farmer: A Millennium Study*.

Bibliography

Bergmann, R.B. 1986. *The Economic Emergency of Women.* New York Inc. Publishers.

Batliwala, S. 1984. "Rural Energy Situation: Consequences for women's health", *Socialist Health Review,* Vol. 1, 2: 72-77.

Bhattacharya, S. 1985. "On the issue of urdernumeration of women's work in the Indian data collection system," in Devaki Jain and N. Banarjee, eds., *Tyranny of the Household: Investigative Essays on Women's Work,* Delhi: Vikas Publishing House Pvt. Ltd.

Bhoite, A. 1987. *Women Employees and Rural Development: Problems of Employed Women in Rural Areas,* Delhi: Gyan Publishing House.

Bieldy, D.D. 1992. "Commitment to work and family." *Annual Review of Sociology,* Vol. 18: 281-302.

Blumstein, P. and S. Pepper. 1983. *American Couples: Money, Work, Sex,* New York: Pocket Books.

Census of India. 1981, Series-28. Delhi: Directorate of Census Operations.

Centre for Women Development Studies. 1984. "Women's Work and Family Strategies: The Indian National Study". Paper Presented in Workshop and Steering Committee Meeting of the Research Scholars on Women's work and Family strategies in South and South East Asia. New Delhi: pp. 1-41.

Chakravarty, I. 1990. "Women and Nutrition" In B. Ray, ed., Women and Science". WSRC series No. 2, Calcutta University: Women's Studies Research Center, pp. 13-29.

Charles, N. and M. Kerr. 1988. *Women, Food and Families,* New York: Manchester University press.

Chatterjee, M. 1988. *Implementing Health Policy,* New Delhi: Manohar Publications.

Dak, R.M. ed., 1988. *Women and Work in Indian Society,* Delhi: Discovery Publishing House.

Dave, C. and K. Sadashivaiah. 1981. "Family size and Quality of Life." *Social Change: Journal of the Council of Social Development,* No. 3 and 4: 35-45.

De, N.R. 1984. "Towards an appreciation of Quality of life and Quality of work life." *Economic and Political Weekly,* 19 (20-21): M46-M57.

Desai, N. and S., Anantram. 1985. "Middle class women's entry into the world of work." In Sardamoni, K., ed., *Women, Work and Society,* Calcutta: Indian Statistical Institute.

Edwards, M., 1981. *Financial Arrangements within Families*. Canberra: National Women's Advisory Council.

Erickson, J.A., Yancey. W.L., and Erickson, E.P. 1979. "Division of family roles," *Journal of Marriage and Family,* Vol. 41: 301-313.

Fox, P.M., and Sharlene. 1984. Hesse-biber. *Women at Work.* 1st edition. Mayfield Publishing Company.

Ghosh, S. 1986. "Discrimination begins at birth." *Indian Pediatrics.* Vol. 23: 51-56.

Goldstein, R.L. 1972. *Indian Women in Transition: A Bangalore Case Study.* Metuchen N. J.: the Scarecrow Press Inc.

Gothaskar, S. ed, 1992. *Struggles of Women at Work.* Delhi: Vikas Publishing House Pvt. Ltd.

Graham, H. 1984. *Women, Health and the Family.* Sussex: The Harvester Press Publishing group.

Gregson, N. and L. Michelle. 1993. "Renegotiating the domestic division of labour: A study of dual career households in North East and South East England." *The Sociological Review.* Vol. 41, 3: 475-505.

Haworth, J.T. and Smith, N.A. ed., 1975. *Work and Leisure.* London: Lepus Books.

Jain, D. and N. Banerjee. 1985. e.d., *Tyranny of the Household: Investigative Essays on Women's Work.* Delhi: Vikas Publishing House Pvt. Ltd.

Kala, R. 1976. *Role Conflict in Working Women.* New Delhi: Chetna Publications.

Kapoor, P. 1974. *The Changing Status of the Working Women in India.* Delhi: Vikas Publishing House Pvt. Ltd.

Kapoor, R., 1969. "Role conflict among employed housewives." *Indian Journal of Industrial Relations,* pp. 39-67.

Kakwani, N. 1987. "Physical Quality of Life indicators and their correlates." Paper presented at World Institute for Development research. Helsinki: Finland, pp. 1-31.

Kumar, R. 1990. *Women's Health, Development and Administration: Principles and Practices*. Vol. II. New Delhi: Deep & Deep Publications.

Leira, A. 1992. *Welfare States and Working Mothers: The Scandinavian Experiences*. Cambridge: Cambridge University Press.

Lin, N. 1976. *Foundations of Social Research*. New York: McGraw-Hill Book Company.

Manheim, H.L. and S. Bradley. 1977. *Sociological Research: Philosophy and Methods*, Illinois: Homewood.

Mathur, D. 1992. *Women, Family and Work*, Jaipur: Rawat Publications.

McLaughlin, D.S. and M.D. Bardara, et. al. ed., 1988. *The Changing Lives of American Women*. Chapel Hill & London: The University of North Carolina Press.

Mechanic, D. 1978. "Sex, Illness, Illness Behaviour and the Health Services." *Social Science and Medicine*. Vol. 12. Serial B.

Mies, M. 1980. *Indian Women and Patriarchy: Conflicts and Dilemmas of Students and Working Women*. New Delhi: Concept Publishing Company.

Miles, I. 1985. *Social Indicators for Human Development*. London: Frances Printer Publishers.

Mills, C.W. 1951. *White Collar: The American Middle Classes*. New York: Oxford University Press.

Miralao, A.V. 1983. "The impact of women's employment on households and family life." Paper presented in Expert Group Meeting on Forward Looking Strategies for the advancement on women. Bangkok.

Myrdal, A. and Klein, V. 1956. *Women's Two Roles: Home and Work.* London: Routledge and Kegan Paul.

National Perspective Plan for Women. 1988-2000 A.D. Report of the Core Group. Department of Women and Child Development. Ministry of Human Resource Development: Govt. of India.

National Sample Survey Organisation. July 1988-June 1989. "Tables with notes on consumer expenditure (All India)." Report. New Delhi: Dept. of Statistics. Govt. of India.

Oakley, A. 1974. *Housewife.* London: Allen Lane.

Olson, D.H. and Brent, C. Miller, ed., 1983. *Family Studies Review Yearbook.* Vol. I. Delhi: Sage Publications.

Pahl, J. 1989. *Money and Marriage.* London: Macmillan.

Parson and Fox. 1991. In Sumaraj, L. e.d., *Women and Medical Care,* Delhi: Ashish Publishing House.

Parthasarthy, J. 1988. "Reasources and Quality of Life: A case study of the Irulas of Nilgiris." *The Eastern Anthropologist.* Vol. 41. July-Sept. 3: 240-249.

Pleck, J.H. 1977. "The work-family role system." *Social Problems.* 24: 417-427.

Rao, A.R. 1988. "Women and Health", Paper in SAARC Guide on Women in Development, India. Prepared by the Women's Development Division, NIPCCD for the Dept. of Women and Child Development,

Ministry of Human Resource Development: Govt. of India, pp. 195-217.

Ross, E.G. and S.D. Raymond. 1975. "Medical Care: Living conditions and children's well-being." *Social Forces*. 61: 456-474.

Safilios-Rothschild, C. 1970. "The study of the family Power structure: A review." *Journal of Marriage and the Family*. Vol. 32: 53-552.

Sathyamala, C.N. Sundharam & N. Bhanot. 1992. *Taking Sides: Issues in Social Medicine and Community Health*. New Delhi: Horizon Indian Books.

Scheer, L. 1980. "Experience with quality of life comparisons." In Szalai, Alexander and P.M. Andrews, e.d., *The Quality of Life: Comparative Studies*. U.S.A.: Sage Publications.

Schuessler, K.F. and G.A. Fisher. 1985. "Quality of Life Research and Sociology." *Annual Review of Sociology*. Vol. 11: 129-208.

Sen, A.K. 1987. "Gender and cooperative conflict." Background Paper for Wider Conference on Poverty, Undernutrition and Living Standards. Helsinki: 27-31 July.

Sethi, R.J. 1978. *Modernization of Working Women in Developing Societies*. Delhi: National Publishing House.

Shah, A.M. 1973. *The Household Dimension of Family in India*. Delhi: Orient Longman.

Simpson, R.L. and H. Simpson. 1981. e.d., *Research in the Sociology of Work: A Research Annual*. Vol. I. INC. Greenwich: Jain Press.

Singh, S. 1993. "Information, money management and marriage" Paper presented to the Fourth Australian Family Research Conference Manly Pacific Parkroyal: 17-19 February.

Smith, B.C. 1979. *Community Health: An Epidemiological Approach*. New York Inc.: Macmillian Publishing Co.

Srivastava, V. 1976. *Employment of Educated Married Women in India: It's Causes and Consequences*. New Delhi: National Publishing House.

Standing, H. 1985. "Women's employment and the household: some findings from Calcutta." *Economic and Political Weekly*, Vol. 20, 17: 23-38.

Suchman, E.A. 1965. "Stages of illness and medical care." *Journal of Health and Human Behaviour*. Vol. 6.

Sumaraj, L. 1991. *Women and Medical Care*. Delhi: Ashish Publishing House.

Szalai, A. and P.M. Andrews. 1980. e.d., *The Quality of Life: Comparative Studies*. U.S.A.: Sage Publications.

Szinovacz, M.E. 1977. "Role allocation, family structure and female employment." *Journal of Mariage and Family*, Vol. 39: 781-91.

Talwar, U. 1984. *Social Profile of Working Women*. Jodhpur: Jain Brothers.

The World's Women: Trends and Statistics. 1979-1990. Social Statistics and Indicators Series K. No. 8. New York: United Nations.

U.N.E.S.C.O. 38. "Indicators of Environmental Quality and Quality of Life." Reports and Papers in the Social Sciences.

Upreti, N. 1988. "The changing status of women in India: Constitutional provisions and social reality."

In Sushila Aggrawal, ed., *Status of Women*. Jaipur: Printwell Publishiers. pp. 13-22.

Vidya, R.G. 1990. *Status of Women Employees in Government*. New Delhi: Mittal Publications.

Yanagisako, S.J. 1979. "Family and Household: The analysis of Domestic Groups." *Annual Review of Anthropology*. Vol. 8: 161-205.

Yoydanoff, P. 1987. *Work and Family Life,* Family Studies Text Series 6: Sage Publications.

Zelizer, V. 1989. 'The Social Meaning of Money: Special Monies", *American Journal of Sociology*: 95(2): 142-377.